The MYSTERY FANcier

Volume 13, Number 4
Fall 1992

The Mystery Fancier

Volume 13, Number 4
Fall, 1992

TABLE OF CONTENTS

MYSTERIOUSLY SPEAKING ...	1
Robert E. Skinner, "An Interview with Ed McBain"	3
Ben Fisher, "Science and Technology in the Writings of Frederick Irving Anderson"	12
Joe R. Christopher, "Father Brown's Final Adventure"	33
Ola Strøm, "The Exit of Father Brown"	42
Marvin Lachman, "The Short Stop"	45
William A.S. Sarjeant, "Crime Novelists as Writers of Children's Fiction: VIII. Dorothy L. Sayers"	53
Maryell Cleary, "The Greatest Misogynist of Them All"	61
William F. Deeck, "The Backward Reviewer"	66
Marvin Lachman, "It's About Crime"	83
VERDICTS (Book Reviews)	95

The Mystery Fancier (USPS: 428-590) is edited and published quarterly by Guy M. Townsend, 2024 Clifty Drive, Madison, IN 47250. William F. Deeck, associate editor; Meredith Phillips, copy editor.

The Mystery Fancier comes to the end of its run with this issue. William F. Deeck, associate editor of TMF during its last years, and invaluable contributor during that period and before, will soon commence publication of his own periodical, *The Criminous Connoisseur*, and any readers who miss *The Mystery Fancier* are strongly urged to give Bill's new journal a try. You're bound to like it. His address is:

William F. Deeck
9020 Autoville Drive
College Park, MD 20740-1302

Copyright 1992 by Guy M. Townsend

Mysteriously Speaking ...

Well, here we are at last, at the end of our run. For the most part it's been fun, and for every part it's been interesting. When I put out the first issue back in 1976 I had never met a real, live mystery fan in the flesh, much less a real, live mystery writer. By the mid-seventies I had made contact with the early enthusiasts of the mystery apa, DAPA-EM, but when that first issue went out I had not yet eye-balled a living and breathing mystery fan except in the mirror every morning.

Sixteen years later I am incalculably richer for having made the acquaintance of hundreds of mystery fans, almost all of whom I like, and dozens of mystery writers, several of whom I like. I have also managed to offend a fair number of individuals and to make steadfast enemies of one or two folks, but I can't say that I'd change much of that even if it were possible. I've been in the wrong more than once—and I've apologized in print and in person more than once—but on balance I don't think I've trampled on too many toes that didn't deserve a good stomping.

In those sixteen years one of the few things that have remained constant in my life has been my love for mysteries, but the many other things in my life that have changed have left me little time to indulge that love. In addition, I have acquired other interests and enthusiasms which compete for my steadily diminishing free time. While I have in actuality devoted very little time to TMF over the past few years, the knowledge that I was neglecting it has kept me from being able to fully enjoy those mysteries that I did steal time to read. Now, with TMF finally put to rest, I hope to be able to rediscover the unmitigated joy that reading a good mystery used to give me.

A word or two of thanks before I go. I won't try to single out individuals, because it would take all the pages of this issue and more just to list them all, and to mention some and not others would not be fair. But I want to say thanks to everyone who made it possible for me to have the delightful privilege of being a mystery fanzine editor and publisher for all these years. Those of us who engage in this crazy activity are always complaining about the time and money that it costs us, but the truth of the matter is that getting to do this work is worth a great deal more to us than what it costs or we just wouldn't do it. So, to all of you who have subscribed to TMF over the years, I thank you for giving me the privilege of doing this. To all of you who have written articles and letters and reviews, I thank you for giving to me, free, things of such great value. And to those of you who have become my friends, who have laughed with me and cried with me, who have listened to and sympathized with me in times of trouble and rejoiced with me in times of triumph, who have—quite unaccountably—honored me with your confidences and your requests for advice, I give to you my thanks, for I have not wealth enough to repay you the true value of what you have given to me.

Go well, my friends. And stay well.

[Bill Deeck writes: "You could mention in "Mysteriously Speaking ..." in the final issue that you will be sending me your mailing list and those on that list will automatically receive the first issue of **The Criminous Connoisseur.** *Should they decide they like it, all they need do is pay for it and they will receive the second issue, and so on until one hopes a regular schedule is adopted and I can go to a subscription basis."]*

An Interview with Ed McBain

Robert E. Skinner

It is likely that if one were to query the many writers of the mystery form known as "police procedural," many of them would say that Ed McBain was their primary literary influence. While there have been many stories and novels over the years that chronicled the exploits of police detectives, the notion of a squad of detectives working together from a single precinct station has to be McBain's original.

McBain was born Salvatore A. Lombino in New York in 1926. He was educated at Cooper Union and Hunter College. After serving in the Navy in World War II, he began writing thrillers and detective stories as well as mainstream novels. As a mainstream writer, he took the name of Evan Hunter and wrote a number of fine mainstream novels, such as *The Blackboard Jungle, Buddwing,* and *Last Summer.* Using this name and those of Curt Cannon, Hunt Collins, Ezra Hannon, and Richard Morrison, he has written well over a hundred novels, countless short stories, screenplays, and even juvenile stories.

In 1956 he tried out a new name, Ed McBain, and wrote a paperback original entitled *Cop Hater.* In this story McBain described the efforts of a hard-working police detective named Steve Carella to uncover three seemingly inexplicable police murders and at the same time win the hand of a beautiful deaf-mute girl named Teddy. He was successful on both counts, and this was the beginning of the saga of the Eighty-Seventh Precinct.

This series, which has gone on now for thirty-five years, boasts an unusual cast of characters that includes a rather philosophical Jewish detective with the unlikely name of Meyer Meyer; Burt Kling, an impetuous younger detective whose love life has had many ups and downs; and even a rather stupid detective named Genarro, who wins his gold shield through a happy blunder. To date there have been forty-two entries in the series, including several volumes of short stories written around the characters.

The series is unique in the annals of crime fiction because McBain has consistently experimented with it. The style has ranged from the sparely hard-boiled to the absurdly comical. Although Steve Carella is the steadiest character and the natural leader, there has never been a single hero in any of the stories. Most of the books chronicle the adventures of more than one cop in the precinct, and two or more unrelated plots are usual.

The stories take place in a fictional city called Isola, although it was clear from the beginning that this is merely a pseudonym for New York City. McBain uses this backdrop to good effect, and the cops in his precinct routinely travel from the ghetto into well-to-do neighborhoods in pursuit of their quarries. The books are richly written, and the joys and sorrows of the various characters are always moving. McBain is a master storyteller who has invested his series with a richness and vitality that would do credit to a mainstream novel.

This interview was originally taped in 1990 to be broadcast over NPR affiliate WWNO–FM in New Orleans. For one reason or another, the interview was never aired, so this appearance is its first.

EM: Oh boy! I didn't feel tired until you mentioned all the things I've written. My God, it seems like a lot, you know. When you do it day by day, however, it doesn't seem so overwhelming.

RES: Have you got a routine that you go through every day? Do you have a set number of pages that you try to get done on a daily basis?

EM: Yeah, I try. When I'm writing a novel, I try for at least ten. Or one day it may be three and the next day it'll be seventeen. Or it'll break down as ten and ten, or five and fifteen, or whatever. But by the end of the week I like to have fifty pages. By the end of the day Friday I like to neaten up all the pages on my desk, tuck everything away, and go home to have a good time for the weekend before I have to come back to work on Monday morning.

RES: Going way back to the beginning of your career, were you really planning on writing a series when you wrote *Cop Hater?*

EM: I had a contract for three books, and it was projected as a series. A realistic series about cops told without frills and with unflinching reality, I hoped. Something that dealt not only with police work but with the human side of the cops, their wives, their children, their girlfriends, their personal disappointments and small triumphs.

RES: I don't recall any American writing prior to your work that can really be described as a police procedural. Were you influenced in the creation of the Eighty-Seventh Precinct series by some other writer, American or foreign?

EM: No, I guess the real influence on the series was not so much literary as it was radio and television. In fact, it was more radio. The only thing I knew about cops before I started researching it for the series was *Dragnet* and other police shows. You know, *Dragnet* was the first show on the air where a cop actually belched. (laughs)

RES: No, I didn't know that. (more laughter)

EM: Or where a cop had a head cold when he was working on a case. And it seemed to me at the time that cops were the same as anybody else except that their profession happens to be law enforcement. So I started with this notion. I don't know if there were any novels before I started the series that dealt with police characters in this way, but I think I was the first, in print, to humanize them. I hate to say that definitely, because there may well have been someone before me.

RES: Well, even if you can't take credit for that, I think it is safe to say that you've certainly influenced a lot of other writers who have written in the procedural form. Even if you're talking about television or the movies, I can remember back in the 1960s shows like *NYPD* that were certainly influenced by your style. These days, of course, we've got one retired cop after another, like Joseph Wambaugh, William Caunitz, and Gerald Petievich. Even though they probably draw to some extent on their own experience, I think one can see that you've influenced all those fellows.

EM: I like to think I may have had some influence on the genre. I don't know if I have or not. I just try to write the best book I know how, and if that's paved the way for other writers in the same field, that's good.

RES: I've always thought that Teddy Carella, Steve's deaf-mute wife, was your most original characterization. How did you conceive of such a character?

EM: I remember the exact moment, you know? It's rare that you can think of the genesis of something, but I remember the exact moment. I was in a car coming home with a friend of mine who was giving me a lift back from the city. I lived in New York at the time, out on Long Island, and he was my next-door neighbor. We were going back home and having dinner with our respective wives. I had just started *Cop Hater,* and we were driving along, both of us wrapped up in our own thoughts, and suddenly I said, "I'm going to make her deaf!" He said, "What?" and I answered, "His wife. The cop's wife. I'm going to make her deaf."

I think the reason it appealed to me so much was that here was a woman who unimpaired people would think of as handicapped. Yet in every way possible, she isn't handicapped. She's beautiful, intelligent, resourceful, and brave. She's a wonderful person in every way, and I thought this would make a terrific character for Steve's wife. And I was also not unaware of the fact that a woman who cannot hear or speak would be in extreme danger if a villain ever came her way.

RES: That's true. You worked that to pretty good effect right in the very first book.

EM: In the first book and in several others. In *The Con Man* I believe that she's trailing the killer as he's about to kill his third victim. I had to be very careful not to turn it into *Mr. and Mrs. North,* you know. So since then, Teddy appears whenever it is necessary for Teddy to appear. But she's not in jeopardy as often as one could be tempted to put her there.

RES: Going back to what I was saying earlier about all these policemen and ex-policemen writing police procedurals, I noticed that really their work doesn't seem a bit more realistic than yours from the professional end. So one would assume that you must really spend an enormous amount of time talking to policemen.

EM: Well, I always envied them a bit, you know. I always envied Joe Wambaugh and Bill Caunitz and Robert Daly and all these writers who have had actual experience in the police department. I guess for them it must be a lot like writing your memories. For me, everything has to come by way of research, snooping around, listening. It's much harder for me to write about cops than it must be for them to do. On the other hand, I think I might have a detachment from it that they don't, and this may have its own value. I can be very humorous about cops. Sometimes I'll write scenes that make it seem like I don't like the characters, when I really do. It may be an advantage, I don't know.

RES: I think it may be. I've noticed the humor in your work that isn't always evident in the work of other writers. Bill Caunitz, for example, is rather humorous, although otherwise his work seems quite realistic. He seems to have created a fantasy cop world in which policemen, all over the world, are a band of brothers for whom getting the job done transcends all other considerations.

EM: Cops do have a kind of fraternal bond. It's a paramilitary organization, and there is this feeling of brotherhood. "We're on the job and it's the good guys versus the bad guys" and all that. Still, I've always felt that my own particular characters were human beings first and cops second, and that's the way I'll always continue to write about them.

RES: Probably one of the toughest things about writing a series of novels about a detective or even a group of detectives is that most writers over the long haul get kind of stale. The characters seem to lose their vibrancy and the stories lose their originality long before the writer reaches the forty-book mark. I'm wondering what kinds of things you have done over the years to try to keep the stories unusual and the characters vibrant and lifelike.

EM: Well, things have happened to the characters over the years and sometimes over the course of a single book. Something that happens in Book D will have repercussions down the line in Book F or G. And I'm not always sure where they will happen. For example, Eileen Burke's rape in *Lightning* is now causing her enormous problems, causing her to go into psychotherapy in *Lullaby*. I still don't know how that's going to be resolved until two or three books down the line.

And I'm so constantly interested in what's happening to these people and how they're changing over the years. They continue to surprise me. Genarro, who is the classic dumbo cop in *Tricks*, the novel before *Lullaby*, suddenly turns into a hero and captures three guys. Andy Parker, the lazy cop who doesn't want to do any work, suddenly cracks a big armed robbery. These things constantly crop up.

In *Lullaby*, for example, Monihan and Monroe, the two homicide cops who are my Tweedle Dum and Tweedle Dee, appear in almost every book where there's a victim at the beginning. They usually make macabre jokes about the corpse's appearance. That she has book legs or "Look, she's wearing white panties," or something like that. Sometimes they'll tell gruesome stories about murders.

In *Lullaby*, which takes place on New Year's Eve, Monihan has been called out from a party and he's slightly drunk. His partner Monroe mentions that "Michael has been out partying," or words to that effect. And the laboratory technician says, "Perhaps that accounts for why you're a little drunk," and Monihan drunkenly says, "I didn't know your first name was Michael," and Monroe says, "Neither did I." Well, the inside joke was that neither did I. This is the fortieth book in the series and Monihan has always been "Monihan," and suddenly I'm surprised to learn that his first name is Michael.

It's these little things that keep it absolutely fresh for me. I never know what's going to happen with these people next. I still don't know how I'm going to resolve this Burt Kling-Eileen Burke conflict. I just don't know how I'm going to resolve it, yet I know that I must.

RES: Well, I'm sure all of Burt's fans will like to see him come away a winner with the ladies just once. He's had more than his share of problems there.

EM: I know. I get so many letters from women saying, "When is that poor boy gonna . . . " "Boy" they call him! "When is that boy going to find happiness?" And I don't know when. Maybe he will, I don't when. I don't deliberately have these women leave him, but they just seem to keep doing it. I like him so much. He's such a nice fellow and a good cop. And he's got a great sense of humor and everything. And yet these women keep leaving him. I don't know why.

RES: You've done some other unusual things over the years. You may be the only writer of realistic police fiction who has used a recurring villain who comes back over and over to plague the detectives. It's kind of a throwback to Rex Stout's Arnold Zeck in the Nero Wolfe stories, isn't it?

EM: Well, even going further back than that, it's a throwback to Professor Moriarty in the Sherlock Holmes stories. I think more than relating to any of those, and again I'm revealing my ignorance of literary forms when I say that the strongest influence on the Eighty-Seventh Precinct series was *Dragnet*. But I'm also revealing my ignorance in stating that I read a lot of comic books when I was a kid. The Joker was a villain who kept coming back to plague Batman. I think the Deaf Man is more closely related to the Joker than he is to Moriarty or any of the other classic literary villains.

RES: In another story I remember that you had fourteen different subplots going on in the same book. That was quite a while back.

EM: That was *Hail, Hail, the Gang's All Here!* wasn't it?

RES: I think it might have been.

EM: Yeah, I had a lot of fun with that one. I just wanted to see how many plots I could juggle in the air and resolve them all by the end of the book. And I wanted to have a case for every member of the squad. So they were all out there plugging away and trying to solve these various cases. I wrote it as if there were two characters, one called "Nightshade" and the other "Daywatch." So it was the night shift, and then we moved into the day shift, or vice versa, I forget which.

RES: Would it be telling for you to let us in on what you're planning to do with the Eighty-Seventh next?

EM: I've already started the book, which will be called *Vespers*, the evening prayer in the Catholic Church. It starts with a priest at his evening prayers who is murdered. There's a little bit of devil worship in it, too. Also I plan to have a resolution of the subplot I started in *Poison*, between Detective Willis and the former hooker.
RES: She's the one that he's protecting from a murder rap, right?
EM: Yeah, she's a murder suspect. And as *Vespers* unravels, we learn that indeed she is a murderer. She has killed someone in Argentina and is wanted for murder down there.
RES: I wish that we could go on talking about this all day. Thanks for spending some time with me.
EM: Thank you. It was a pleasure. ♦

Science and Technology in the Writings of Frederick Irving Anderson

Ben Fisher

I.

Frederick Irving Anderson (1877–1947), once well-known to readers of popular American literary periodicals (particularly *The Saturday Evening Post*) during the first half of this century, is best remembered for his crime stories and the several groups of series characters who enlivened them: the "infallible" Godahl and the "notorious" Sophie Lang, two endearing rogues (so endearing in Sophie's case that three films were made of her exploits during the 1930s); Deputy Inspector Parr, of New York City's Detective Police Force; his friend, Oliver Armiston, the "extinct author" (extinct because one of his crime stories had provided a criminal his model for an actual crime and thereafter the police forced Armiston to stop writing fiction); their two assistants, the handsome, suave, redheaded Morel and the shabby, seemingly dimwitted, little Pelts, who, however, never allowed his quarry to escape; and, finally, the hard-working, shrewd and witty New Englanders, Jason Selfridge and Constable Orlando Sage, whose efforts were combined with those of Armiston and Parr to maintain law and order in stories from Anderson's later years.

Surveyed entire, however, Anderson's publications reveal considerable displays in the way of science and technology, which were advancing at an astounding rate within the time of his literary career. His early activities in newspaper journalism may have stimulated his interests in these phenomena, and the advertisements for scientific-technological materials and literature peppered across pages of the periodicals for which he wrote make us aware how rich a treasure house of popular-culture materials these fields had come to be by the early years of the twentieth century. Behind the popularizing impulses lay the vast legacies of nineteenth-century science, not to mention the curiosity about all sorts of learning and culture of an ever-growing reading public.

That a writer aspiring to master a market and to retain an audience would turn to science and technology for assistance is therefore entirely understandable. In these respects, after all, Anderson was but emulating such worthy predecessors in crime fiction as Nathaniel Hawthorne, Edgar Allan Poe, or Wilkie Collins, as well as Arthur Conan Doyle and many more from the gaslight era that immediately preceded Anderson's own emergence on the literary scene. Among his contemporaries and successors in this vein, we may number Sax Rohmer, S. S. Van Dine, Anthony Berkeley, John Dickson Carr, and Ian Fleming. Furthermore, we may need to be reminded, as Patrick Moore comments, that it "would be wrong to suggest that all science fiction descends from the horror comics and the 'pulp magazines' of the 1930's."[1]

---

1. I discuss several of these matters in *Frederick Irving Anderson (1877-1947): A Biobibliography* (Madison, Indiana: Brownstone Books, 1987; San Bernardino, California: Borgo Press, 1988), pp. 9-10. J.A.V. Chapple provides an excellent panorama of relevant linkages in *Science and Literature in the Nineteenth Century* (London: Macmillan, 1986). For parallels in terms of Poe's practices that demonstrate an alertness to current scientific activities—which often verged on fads—see Charles K. Wolfe, "Poe and the Romance of Science," *The Romantist*, 2 (1978), 37-39; Clive Bloom et al., eds., *Nineteenth-Century Suspense from Poe to*

II.

A brief glance at Anderson's nonfiction writings, which demonstrate his initial attempts in the literary—as distinguished from the strictly news-columnist—milieu, may well occupy our attention before we focus on his stories and novelettes.

His first signed essay, "The Man Who Heard Voices," in *Harper's Weekly* for 15 February 1908 (pp. 10-12), treats the career of Frank W. Sandford, whose purported communications with the other world, principally with God, led to establishment of "The Holy Ghost and Us" sect in Maine. Anderson brings terminology from psychology to bear upon Sandford's magnetic powers in drawing followers to his causes, noting that the prophet might be termed a "paranoiac" by his opponents.

Air travel provided the topic for Anderson's next article, "The French Think Wilbur Wright Is a Bird," also in *Harper's Weekly* (24 October 1908, p. 30). Not only the experiments of the Wright brothers, but the efforts of Zeppelin, in Germany, furnish the centers of interest in this discourse on aircraft.

Anderson later concentrated on another scientific-technological aid to better living in America, that of systematized agriculture, in *The Farmer of Tomorrow*. Portions of this book appeared first in *Everybody's Magazine,* one of the popular periodicals of the times, during 1912 and 1913, and, expanded, in hardcover form in the

---

Conan Doyle (New York: St. Martin's Press, pp. 93-94, 108—on Doyle's uses of scientific elements and on German and American outdistancing of Britain in technology in the nineteenth century—and David Ketterer, *New Worlds for Old: The Apocalyptic Imagination, Science Fiction, and American Literature* (Bloomington: Indiana University Press, 1974), pp. 15-25. Moore's cautionary note appears in *Science and Fiction* (London: George G. Harrap, 1957), p. 9. For ready assistance to my work, I thank James E. Rocks, Lance Schachterle, Sara E. Selby, and Julie A. Fisher.

latter year. Crop rotation and other, then new, methods for soil conservation were discussed.

That astonishing scientific-technological advance in American civilization, electricity practically applied, likewise commanded Anderson's fascination and respect. In a second agricultural book, *Electricity for the Farm* (1915), he provided sensible, straightforward information as to labor savings and conveniences becoming available from electric current, principally that derived from water power.

Another technological development, in transportation, prompted him to recommend electric engines for use in automobiles in hopes of achieving greater efficiency and preventing pollution. Surely this writer should be worth the attention of today's conservationists, ecologists, and antipollutionists. His article on this topic, "The Automobilist's Dream," appeared, tellingly enough, in the *Scientific American* for 13 January 1917 (p. 61), when the auto-filled highways of today were not yet even envisioned.

Along like lines of anticipating some of our contemporary technological minuses, Anderson suggested elsewhere how, taking a lesson from fiddler ants, humans might save time and money (though money would not have bedeviled the industrious insects) by growing their own food instead of expending energies and expense in transporting it (*Everybody's Magazine*, 29 [May 1913], 656-657).

III.

These examples indicate Anderson's shiftings from areas of hard, empiric science into those of speculative dimensions. After all, not every subscriber to popular magazines or newspaper-fiction supplements, like those which ran his articles and stories, nor each reader of his agricultural books, would necessarily subscribe wholeheartedly to the newfangled concepts marshalled in those publications, much less the how-to-do-it instructions set forth in the two books on modernized farming.

Anderson himself expressed what was surely a widespread skepticism toward a too-literal acceptance of science in his repeated use in fiction of the term "scientifico" as one of amusement when referring to persons engaged in many occupations linked with science and technology. Those targeted often came from the ranks of doctors involved in police crime research, the coroners and toxicologists who explained many a mystery to the impatient, unlettered Deputy Parr. Parr's investigations often depended not nearly so much on what he himself possessed in the way of scientific knowledge as on information given him by others. Just so, his fellow delver into crime, Oliver Armiston, furnished intuitive scope to the bulldog tenacity and ape-like physiognomy and psychology of the great deputy inspector.

Anderson's crime tales drew upon aspects of technology and science that would simultaneously stimulate but not overwhelm the minds of readers of, say, *The Saturday Evening Post, Everybody's,* or fiction supplements in the *Chicago Tribune,* where his writings circulated. Obviously, such audiences did not customarily have at their fingertips a detailed knowledge of theoretical science, nor, in the main, even much applied science, and they had no wish for oversupplies of details that might diminish the impact of dramatic criminal activity unfolding on the pages before them. In a noncrime story, "The Siamese Twins" (*Saturday Evening Post,* 8 February 1919), the "science of physiognomy," according to a clothier, encompasses all aspects of dress and grooming. An additional remark, "I understand janitors make scientific study of a tenant's garbage bucket —curator of dumb-waiter bones, so to speak," maintains a lightness of outlook on the subject that would doubtless appeal to a mass reading audience (p. 34).

Fittingly, in the light of his critics' generalized labeling him as a crime-fiction writer (although his wares were varied), Anderson's stories began to appear in a magazine entitled *Adventure,* in 1911 and 1912, when medical knowledge, upon which he drew time and again, had in no way grown so sophisticated as subsequent advances have made present-day accomplishments in the field. In what might have proved to be a promising series (except that Anderson did not choose to keep using his first sleuth for very long), Mr. White, who was associated with the New York Police Force, tackled several mysterious deaths in which medical awareness proved to be of paramount importance.

First, in "The Unknown Man" (*Adventure,* 2 [August 1911], 645-650), White reveals that what seemed to be a death by drowning was actually a murder effected by means of a cocaine injection, administered by Dr. Drud to a victim whose name is never specified—thus the "unknown man" of the title. Drud and the newspaper editor, Bryson, engage in the major portions of dramatic dialogue that give this story its structure. White's case is clinched by a surgical supplier's information that the broken part of the needle used in the killing was part of a product made especially for Drud. Interestingly, Anderson's last story to be published, "The Man from the Death House," reworks this same theme (*Ellery Queen's Mystery Magazine,* 17 [January 1951], 82-95).

Another Mr. White story, "The Purple Flame," reveals how cyanide poisoning, accomplished by means of a match doctored to release deadly gas when ignited, took of the life of Mr. Potter, who had broken up the marriage of chemist Homer Jaffray (*Adventure,* 5 [November 1912], pp. 11-17; rpt. *Ellery Queen's Mystery Magazine,* 13 [January 1949], 112-121).

Elsewhere we observe that medicine functions in other ways as a major theme in one of Anderson's two novelettes, "An Hour of Leisure" (serialized in the *Saturday Evening Post,* July-August 1914). Elderly Major Beeston betrays symptoms of heart trouble, his pulse rate and dosage of digitalis are discussed, and a principal character is his physician, Dr. Sarny, whose alertness to Beeston's "tell-tale grayish pallor" spurs the young medical practitioner to stay on the case for financial gain.

In this respect he resembles (but pallidly, without their colorful personalities) Count Fosco, Dr. Candy, or Dr. Downward—respectively in Wilkie Collins's *The Woman in White, The Moonstone,* and *Armadale*—who are not above misusing their medical knowledge and skills. These characters are similar in their proud boasts concerning their abilities in medicine. Just so, in *The Scarab Murder Case,* S. S. Van Dine devotes an entire chapter—Ch. 11, "The Coffee Percolator"—to the finer points of coffee brewing, by what in 1930 were not yet common methods, to reveal ultimately that opium-laced coffee had been used deliberately to drug Dr. Bliss.

Anderson seems to have notable antipathies toward medical persons who abused their training in the interests of crime. In this respect he shares the outlook of another, earlier, American author—and one unlikely to come to mind immediately for fans of crime fiction—William Cullen Bryant, whose interest in medicine and advances in evolutionary theory were great, but who disliked dabblers or pseudoscientists.[1]

Anderson, however, is much more in the mainstream of American literature overall than has generally been remarked, as I will note again below, and so such attitudes are not surprising. In a lighter vein as regards medical men than we find in "An Hour of Leisure," we read in "The Flame in the Socket" (*Saturday Evening Post,* 26 February 1919, p. 26) that a dying man is visited by doctors, "to study him under the microscope of their science—and to warn him in a purely academic way to walk the chalk line,

---

1. Charles I. Glicksburg, "William Cullen Bryant and Nineteenth Century Science," *New England Quarterly,* 23 (March 1950), 91-96.

that he might not accidentally break off the point they had whittled away to such a nicety."

Cyanide poisoning, to return to that means for murder (and one which, apparently, preoccupied Anderson the detective-fictionist), is used once again with equal or greater subtlety in a later story, "Beyond All Conjecture" (*Saturday Evening Post*, 29 September 1928, pp. 12-13, 48ff.; rpt. *The Book of Murder*, pp. 1-33). Old Cornelius Vlemynck dies after licking a cyanide-impregnated envelope glue. Deputy Parr learns about this cause of death from a police toxicologist, and the rest of the story revolves around analyses of inks, watermarks, type fonts, typewriter models, and photographic chemicals. Those last substances darkened the fingernails of the murderer and thus provided the clue that brought him to justice.

Perhaps as a sop to readers who would look askance at science used so prominently in a crime story, the analyses are designated "voodoo." Sherlock Holmes, we may remember, had studied variances in tobacco ash, although his work in that line is merely mentioned without elaboration. Armiston, significantly, comments in terms of psychological aberration upon the murderer's burning desire to annihilate his victim, and so he draws into the fabric of this story another kind of science.

Cyanide gas intended as a murder weapon recurs in "The Half-Way House," this time as an instrument of fratricide (*American Magazine*, 93 [May 1922], 48-51; rpt. *Ellery Queen's Mystery Magazine*, 11 [February 1948], 132-143; *Ellery Queen's Mid-Year Anthology*, 5 [1963], 119-131). An engineer figures among those who eventually clear up the mystery, which meantime carries suggestions of supernaturalism.

Such blendings of quasi-supernaturalism, misapplied science, and detection occur in some interesting forerunners of Anderson's methods. For example, the spectral "eye" that so haunts the baronet in L. T. Meade's "The Horror of Studley Grange," in *Stories from the Diary of a Doctor* (1894), proves to be a carefully calculated and manipulated optical device intended to drive its victim to premature death. A similar deviousness on the part of a scientist occurs in Stapleton's use of phosphorous to impart apparently otherworldly fearsomeness to his large beast in Doyle's *The Hound of the Baskervilles* (1902). Intermittent suggestions of supernaturalism combine with murder involving poisoned cigarettes in S. S. Van Dine's *The Gracie Allen Murder Case* (1938), where, however, the prolonging of the revelation of the truth grows wearisome.

Late in his own literary career, in "Murder in Triplicate," Anderson alludes to murder by cyanide poisoning in an unmistakably wry tone, as if he were aware of its too-repetitive use in crime stories, and, maybe, as if he wished to separate actuality from any hint of supernaturalism. From Deputy Parr come these words: "There are methods [of committing murder], as you know, that elude even such an avid dissectionist as our medical examiner. The fashionable one, just now, in detective fiction, is to produce an embolism by injecting an air or gas bubble into an artery. Cyanide has rather gone out—it leaves its trace—and in real life it takes more of the stuff than in fiction" (*Ellery Queen's Mystery Magazine,* 8 [December 1946], 79).

A different, but equally gripping, approach appears in the brief but hard-hitting allusion to scientific developments that opens "The Touch on His Shoulder," a spy story (*McClure's Magazine,* 50 [March 1918], 20ff.). The astounding devastation wrought on the European theater of battle in World War I through the consequences of experimental, improved military technology provides the scenic and thematic effects for the opening paragraph of the story. A shop window display presents a gripping visual of destruction and ghastly suffering:

> It was a photograph of No-Man's land . . . It was horrible in its details—the torn earth, the shattered stumps of trees, the gro-

> tesque heaps of dead under the rains, the sleet, and the torrid suns, denied even the decency of turning to clay. Over them bullets searched endlessly; a pall of suffocating gas was wafted by the wind in greenish blighting vapors; now the troubled earth would be rent with some fresh cataclysm, churning the inert mass as if these were denied peace even in their long sleep, as if some greedy monster feared they were not yet sufficiently dead. But they were dead. Some for weeks, or months, lying out there under the sky. To some it had come swiftly, the transition of an instant across the dividing line; to others, slowly, helplessly, while they groaned for succor that could not come, or cursed their stubborn blood for prolonging life. (p. 20)

The lengthy remainder of the story never again returns to such graphic horrors, but this beginning lays the groundwork for the crushing, and similarly horrifying, psychological torments sustained by a no longer useful German spy as he draws nearer to the fitting and sensational ending of his own life.

As might be expected in crime fiction today, fingerprinting in Anderson's stories plays a signal role in foiling criminals' plans. Readers of the 1920s would have found this type of evidence somewhat less commonplace, although Conan Doyle and R. Austin Freeman had given extended treatment to forging such evidence, respectively, in "The Adventure of the Norwood Builder" (1904) and *The Red Thumb Mark* (1907). We may also profitably recall, at this juncture, Poe's Dupin discoursing on the weird large fingerprints—of the orangutan—in "The Murders in the Rue Morgue." Anderson's Mr. White quite early solved the mystery of a would-be diamond theft by using tactics from this branch of detective work ("Beyond a Reasonable Doubt," *Adventure,* 4 [October 1912], 67-74).

Anderson seemingly found fingerprints fascinating; they recur in "The Phantom Alibi," along with handwriting analysis (*McClure's Magazine,* 52 [November 1920], 27-28; rpt. *Ellery Queen's Mystery Magazine,* 10 [November 1947], 87-99), in the first of Sophie Lang's adventures

("The Signed Masterpiece," *McClure's Magazine*, 52 [June-July 1921], 21-23ff; rpt. *The Notorious Sophie Lang*, pp. 1-37; *Ellery Queen's Mystery Magazine*, 4 [November 1943], 78-98)—where, in fact, an absence of fingerprints intensifies police suspicions against Sophie; in "Finger Prints," a story about how evidence of the law's setting aside of evidence from those telltale marks—which reads like a parody of detective stories (*Saturday Evening Post*, 23 October 1926, pp. 16-17ff.); and in "Thumbs Down," one of Anderson's last *Saturday Evening Post* stories (28 June 1930, pp. 10-11ff.). In a novel of just slightly later date, *Darkness at Pemberley* (1932), T. H. White would include compelling information concerning the finer points of fingerprint study, detailed by the murderer himself.

Shifting into a different field, Anderson produced two stories concerning thievery of gold by liquefying it. The chemical processes of maintaining the precious metal in liquid form are explained in each ("The Fifth Tube," *Saturday Evening Post*, 13 December 1913, pp. 16-17ff.; rpt. *Adventures of the Infallible Godahl*, pp. 161-193; "Murder in Triplicate," *Ellery Queen's Mystery Magazine*, 8 [December 1946], 75-87). In the first story, the great rogue Godahl siphons away the valuable fluid and transforms it into a decorative frieze in his home; in the second, notable attention goes toward describing the grotesque purple spotting on the hands of those working with the substance. In both stories, we encounter elements of mystery and grotesquerie that ultimately turn out to be founded upon very plausible, if unusual, circumstances. The Godahl story concludes on a humorous note as the suave con man revels in the splendors of his opulent appointment.

"Murder in Triplicate," with its allusion to Poe's "imp of the perverse" (p. 83), might alert us to a possible Andersonian recollection of Poe's manipulation of alchemy in "Von Kempelen and His Discovery." Furthermore, ballistic analysis in Anderson's story also descends, whether indirectly or not, from Poe's parodic detective tale, "Thou Art the Man," which also combines science and detection. In Anderson's "The Alchemists," the attempted smuggling of actual coins, concealed in crates beneath lead type fonts, gives another twist to ramifications of "alchemy" (*Saturday Evening Post*, 2 January 1915, pp. 8ff.). Astronomy also figures, if with mere brush strokes, in several of Anderson's stories, e. g. "The Follansbee Imbroglio." In all of these, given the fortunes in literature of alchemists and astronomers, we encounter Andersonian modifications of Gothic tradition.

Along similar lines, telegraphy and the telephone, phonograph equipment and wiretapping (these last in "The Golden Fleece," *Saturday Evening Post,* 4 May 1918, pp. 20-21ff.), reiterated use of and calling attention to automobiles—and even the "suddenly interrupted scenes of some moving-picture screen," in 1914, when cinema was still in its embryonic stages ("The Man Who Couldn't Go Home," *Saturday Evening Post,* 28 March 194, pp. 17-19ff.): all are employed to make those stories appeal to readers on bases of their timely technology. Scouts for the movies are also mentioned in "An Hour of Leisure," already cited in another context, in which a young man meets an attractive girl while attending a movie.

Parr and Armiston confront yet other kinds of new machines, namely the telephone and a Dictaphone, in "The Follansbee Imbroglio," a novelette serialized in the *Saturday Evening Post* (29 July and 5 August 1922). The phone, in its then imperfect state, is cited for the kind of "cross-talking" that here so closely resembles the "language" overheard by witnesses in Poe's "The Murders in the Rue Morgue." The demonstration of the Dictaphone seems to the hearers to be the "hocus-pocus" of a "pseudo séance" (Part Two, p. 30), and thus, and much more entertainingly than in "The Man Who Heard Voices," discussed above, the Victorian popular pastime of spiritualism is amusingly laid to rest by modern technology.

"The Ivory Hunters" (*Saturday Evening Post*, 28 October 1916, pp. 17ff.), a crime story without a detective, opens with a vignette about the vastnesses of a skyscraper elevator system, which Anderson makes analogous to a railroad, with appropriate "expresses and locals and specials, and semaphores and red-and-green signal lights, as well as conductors, engineers, starters and a timetable" (p. 17). This is evidently Anderson's gambit to make recent technology comprehensible to audiences who probably would have had far greater acquaintance with railroads than with intricate elevator operations.

Such a beginning also lays proper technical groundwork for a story that takes us from a tall office building in New York City (replete with the latest technology) to a small rural Western community, birthplace of Sam Burnell, a typical American literary character in his moving thence—after an episode in swindling made life too hot for him—to the big city and its furtherance of his criminal habits. Highly mechanized elevators are of no use to Sam once he re-enters his hometown to try yet another mountebank sham, conniving to gain control of the power-and-light association in the area for his own business firm.

Although the small-town businessmen have become well acquainted with "power houses, converting stations, gas plants, repair shops . . . strings of high-tension transmission lines, double and single track railroads with their spurs, to handle the short-haul freight, and great trunk mains for gas and water," and ticker-tape recorders, they had not altogether lost their primitive dynamism, either. Sam Burnell is whipped thoroughly in a fistfight to the blood with hometowner Henry Haig and then sent packing after he has been "persuaded" to donate generously to a new athletic park for the town's boys. Although this vignette of combat smacks strongly of Tom Sawyer's antics, it also anticipates the definitely more brutal hand-to-hand encounters in the oncoming hard-boiled school of American crime fiction and the violence that would provide thrills in American movie theaters.

Another adventure of a young Midwesterner who moves to the beckoning but wicked city of New York to try his luck there, and who, ironically, is preserved from ill fortune by none other than the Infallible Godahl, is that of Moberly Grimsy, in "An Hour of Leisure," already mentioned. Here details of the mechanics of newspaper printing, a safecracker's tool (compared with a physician's stethoscope), electric alarms, fire engines, and medicine are blended splendidly with hints of magic, ghosts, and penny dreadfuls to maintain readers' interest.[1]

A nondetective story from this same period, "The Unknown Masterpiece" (*Saturday Evening Post*, 5 June 1915, pp. 10-11ff.), centers upon attempts to make a surreptitious recording on wax disks of pianist Jacoby's matchless music, in which the musician outwits the manager, Orson Merlin. The name Merlin may also signal blends of technology and magic in line with long-held traditions regarding the wily sage whose role in Arthurian lore shifted, depending on the version encountered and regardless of varieties of "spells" he casts (the story offers ambiguous hints in this respect). Ironically—but in genuine Andersonian fashion—the technology engaged by the man with the magician's name ultimately proves powerless in the face of musician Jacoby's idealistic persistence in denying as his the piece Merlin recorded. Anderson's potential cognizance of Poe's Dupin's balancing the poet with the mathematician, or emotion with rationalism, may also come into play in this story.

---

1. Clarence Gohdes, "Wicked Old New York," *Huntington Library Quarterly*, 24 (February 1966), 171-181.

Anderson's chief characters are akin to types that became stereotypical as science-fiction figures. Mr. White, Godahl, Sophie Lang, Armiston, and Parr: all embody characteristics of the overreacher. Their ancestry in Sherlock Holmes (and his sidekick, Dr. Watson, as well as that wily antagonist, Professor Moriarty), Poe's Dupin, and Dr. Victor Frankenstein may be readily traced. Like hosts of other mad scientists, those of Hawthorne, say, Anderson's evil doctors (he seems to have harbored noticeable antipathies toward scientists or technologists gone wrong) come to bad ends like suicide or the death penalty meted out by law courts. Thus Anderson blends fiction with developments in science and technology somewhat in the manner of Oscar Wilde's *The Picture of Dorian Gray* (1890, 1891). There, a chemist's abilities are requisitioned to destroy the body of murdered Basil Hallward; the chemist's remorse drives him to take his own life as well.

In this respect, Anderson's warped scientists foreshadow some of the more cosmically oriented evil geniuses created later in the century. Two good examples come from 1940s serial films: the crazed Dr. Tobar, who threatens Jack Armstrong, and the world, with an all-consuming blowup if his wishes are balked; and the nefarious Crimson Ghost (a disguised professor of science), who desires to control the world by means of negatively directed atomic power. These fellows were related to many other diabolic figures in fiction, past and present. One is never certain about the borders over which science and technology merge with detective fiction, especially since they share a common lineage in Gothicism.

Moreover, Anderson casts his evil scientists such that they become reminiscent of another favorite American literary type, the confidence man. Anderson's hoaxers often prove to be as savage in their varieties of duplicity as Poe's (or Melville's). The narrators in "The Tell-Tale Heart" and "The Black Cat," Montresor in "The Cask of Amontillado," or the Minister D—— in "The Purloined Letter" may well stand as ancestors to Anderson's Dr. Drud, young Vlemynck, Homer Jaffray, and Wolfbane in "Gulf Stream Green." Anderson draws nearly all of these strands together, although his expertly woven whole cloth carries subtle designs that put forth no single characteristic too stridently. The Infallible Godahl and Sophie Lang, we recall, manifest wholly different sets of con-artist habits.

A trait that differentiates him from many of his predecessors in crime fiction is that Anderson's scientists, "mad" or otherwise, don't employ their abilities for sexual satisfaction or deviation, except, perhaps, in the divorce theme underlying "The Purple Flame."[1] Not necessarily a mad scientist, old Major Beeston, in that story where reality and apparent magic combine in a plausible manner, "An Hour of Leisure," is marked as a descendant of Gothic types because of his "devilishly discerning eye," his "all-seeing eye of the master." As if to heighten such apparently evil intents, he is also characterized as an Eastern potentate with an "impaling" brow.

IV.

Frederick Irving Anderson's command of scientific and technological knowledge, as I trust I have shown, found deft uses in his literary endeavors. Moving from primarily factual planes of science and their potential benefits to humankind, he altered such positive features frequently in his fiction to create suspense and to make readers aware that negative, criminal, results were likely to occur when elements from the sciences and technology were calculatedly mishandled. Anderson's stories are not the type of

---

1. See, for examples of such desires, Taylor Stoehr's *Hawthorne's Mad Scientists: Pseudoscience and Social Science in Nineteenth-Century Life and Letters* (Hamden, Conn.: Archon Books, 1978), pp. 47–49, 53–58, 260–264.

science fiction that dramatizes clashes between opposing planets, nor do his monsters appear in animal or vegetable guises. Instead, and like those connected with the fearsome Hound of the Baskervilles, Anderson's terrors have altogether realistic foundations, and they are of the sorts that the average reader of his day (and even our day, if we take into account time's changes of the American civilization profile since the earlier twentieth century) could comprehend as such.

With no aim to give us wars of worlds, Anderson, rather, offers us, like the Romantic poet, Wordsworth, an extraordinariness that is not at all far removed from ordinariness. Medicine, mathematics, physics, engineering, telephones, submarine telegraph, bridge construction, automobiles, the movies, phonographs, books on house flies: these constituted the fascinating, the unfamiliar, and the ambivalent in his day. His writings about such phenomena give him a place in the big picture of American literary expression, according to David Ketterer's perceptions of the mergers between science fiction and American literature overall (pp. 15-25).

Such incorporations of these areas into literature as we find in Anderson's fiction suggest that he was trying to draw together two modes in presenting science and technology through the medium of crime fiction. The first of these intentions is well expressed in words found in Herman Melville's novel, *White Jacket:* ". . . a man of true science . . . uses but few hard words, and those only when none others will answer his purpose; whereas the smatterer in science . . . thinks that by mouthing hard words, he proves that he understands hard things."

This phraseology might describe Jason Selfridge, who reappears in several stories after his debut in "The Golden Fleece." Regardless of his "degree in technology" and his skills as an auto mechanic, he returns to his New England country home for summer haying. A man of few words, but jocular withal, Jason conveys a strong sense of his unassuming understanding of hard things.

Another man of few words, and about the sourest among Anderson's gallery of characters, old Ezra Beddes in "Wild Honey," when he permits himself to dream, has visions of "cogs and pawls and ratchets and whirring pinions" (*Saturday Evening Post*, 26 November 1921, p. 6). The whirring of an electric separator, operated after morning milking by his son, in a nearby shed, catches his ear. Other noises—of a defective auto cylinder, of a saw, of hauling grain—these are the poetry of his existence. Later he thinks that the flight of a bee resembles that of an airplane. Anderson subtly sets this technological plane, with deft touches, to throw into bolder relief, later, events dogged by rural superstitions related to death.

Likewise, "The Fifth Tube" begins arrestingly by quoting, from "the pharmacopoeia," that "the size of the drops of different liquids bears no relation to their density; sulphuric acid is stated by Durand to yield ninety drops to the fluid drachm, while water yields but forty-five, and oil of anise, according to Professor Procter, eighty-five. It follows, then, that the weight of the drop varies with most liquids; but few experiments of this subject have been recorded, the oldest being contained in Mohr's Pharmacopoeia of 1845. More accessible to the American and English student are the results of Bernoulli" (*Saturday Evening Post*, 13 December 1913, pp. 16–17ff.; rpt. *Adventures of the Infallible Godahl*, pp. 161–193). Combined with Godahl's calculations and conversations, which immediately follow, the effect upon readers—that before them on the page were revealed great scientific propositions —is one of admission to intimacy with deep learning.

"The Mad Hour" (*McClure's Magazine,* 50 (June 1918), 13ff.), in a similar manner, opens with the statement that an "equation is a beautiful thing: it is the law of compensation balanced to a hair" (p. 13). Before that story concludes, the sciences of biology and physics are drawn in, with references to Luther Burbank and Mendel's experiments with plants. Poetry and science team to create a compelling opening paragraph in "The Assassins," one of Anderson's stories about the New York theater world—one in which appear appropriate allusions to motifs from the Eastern milieu of the Arabian Nights, with its mixtures of romance and death-dealing reality (*Pictorial Review*, 22 [February 1921], 12–13ff.).

Stories like these reveal Anderson's ways of bringing scientific-technological learning into the homes of America's magazine readers. These were the very people who would understand what he meant by labeling as "scientists" the readers of electric meters or inspectors of water spigots. ("The Signed Masterpiece," *McClure's Magazine*, 52 [June/July 1921], 22). The same audiences, too, would without difficulty have comprehended possible unpleasant results of bungled experiments—like the death of wealthy Amos P. Huntington, an amateur who blew himself up in seeking to create synthetic rubber, mentioned in the same story. Those same readers might have taken Frederick Irving Anderson to their hearts for his desire to keep alive his experience at such handicrafts as the making of an axe handle by using another axe to carve it, or his knowledge of milking cows by hand.[1] Both sides would have little truck with mere "mouthing" as that remarked above.

---

1. "The Dead End," *Saturday Evening Post*, 29 December 1923, p. 12; rpt. *The Book of Murder*. Elsewhere Jason's pursuits reveal features of the city mouse–country mouse motif. Thus we find Anderson in yet another way incorporating long-recognized elements of American humor into his crime stories; cf. my book, cited in n 1 above, pp. 5–6; and my "Frederick Irving Anderson and the Infallible Godahl," *Clues*, 9:2 (Fall/Winter 1988), 15–17. Anderson's handwork on the farm is described in Charles Honce, *Mark Twain's Associated Press Speech and Other New Stories on Murder, Modes, Mysteries, Music and Makers of Books* (New York: Privately Printed, 1940), pp. 53–56.

Anderson's second method was anticipated by none other than Sherlock Holmes himself, who admonishes Watson: "Detection is, or ought to be, an exact science and should be treated in the same cold and unemotional manner. You have attempted to tinge it with romanticism." This upbraiding, which occurs in Chapter One of *The Sign of Four*, might with equal force have been directed at Anderson. In his stories, the ways of the scientist and technologist are made palatable for the untrained American readership of the popular periodicals. Of course, Holmes's grapplings with the perils of misapplied science and technology were often tinged with a romanticism that emanated from the sleuth himself and not from his more mundane companion. Watson later compliments Holmes, as if to mollify him, for bringing "detection as near an exact science as it will ever be brought in this world."

Like Arthur Conan Doyle, Frederick Irving Anderson gives us fiction with zestful overlays of science and technology—more of the latter, perhaps—rather than dry factual blueprints for solutions to crimes. Like his countryman of an earlier era, Charles Brockden Brown, often dubbed the "father of the American novel" or "the first American Gothic novelist," Anderson is typically American in creating horrors at once exaggerated and scientifically mechanical. In attempting to become popular, he created a set of characters whose knowledge and uses of science and technology were such that an audience could locate convincing values there; that is, readers could identify with those who employed the fields rightly, toward positive ends, and maintain their distance from those on the negative side.

Writing as he did, Anderson also fulfilled expectations in the editorial statement by the *Saturday Evening Post* that fiction published there "deals with American subjects and the people of today accurately." Frederick Irving Anderson's writings—with their recurrent features of science and technology and the tone of healthy skepticism and wry, balanced reasoning sounded when circumstances called for viewing the extremes to which technology or science might be carried (from an author whose allegiance to advances in those areas did not make him forget the value of less sophisticated, manual labor)—frequently recall to us that only in the seventeenth century was "literature" separated from "science," and that time-honored traditions had not so divided them.[1] He certainly betrays no inclination to split one from the other.

In the manner of one of his literary predecessors, Benjamin Franklin, Anderson brought into American homes theoretical and practical knowledge of the world surrounding them, and that information arrived within an entertaining framework. ◆

---

1. Brigid Brophy, "Detective Fiction: A Modern Myth of Violence," *Hudson Review*, 18 (Spring 1965), 11-30, notes that Sherlock Holmes "touch[es], but only lightly, on technology"; compare Stanton O. Berg, "Sherlock Holmes: Father of Scientific Crime Detection," *The Armchair Detective*, 5:2 (January 1972, 81-87, 90. See also David S. Reynolds, *Beneath the American Renaissance: The Subversive Imagination in the Age of Emerson and Melville* (New York: Alfred A. Knopf, 1988), p. 240; William Hazlitt, "American Literature," *Edinburgh Review*, 50 (October 1829), 126-127. See also Stephen Knight, "The Case of the Great Detective," *Meanjin Quarterly*, 40:2 (July 1981), 175-185. The policy statement is quoted from William B. McCourties, *Where and How to Sell Manuscripts* (1919), by James B. Meriwether in "Faulkner Corresponds with *The Saturday Evening Post*," *Mississippi Quarterly*, 30 (Summer 1977), 462, n5. The distancing of literature from science is examined in E. S. Shaffer, "Literature and Science: Towards a New Literary History," *University of Hartford Studies in Literature*, 19:1 (1987), 37-47.

Father Brown's Final Adventure

Joe R. Christopher

In 1991 the final Father Brown short story was published—the fifty-third, if the prologue and epilogue of *The Secret of Father Brown* are counted separately and "The Donnington Affair" half story is also counted (see Peterson, "A Father Brown Bibliography," Part One, 39-43). This ultimate story, "The Mask of Midas," so far as is known, was not published in G. K. Chesterton's lifetime. The manuscript does bear the inscription "New Series, No. 2," meaning that it followed "The Vampire of the Village" for an intended sixth volume of Father Brown stories. "The Vampire of the Village" was published in 1936, the year of Chesterton's death. But Chesterton died, and Dorothy Collins, his secretary, chose for whatever reason not to publish "The Mask of Midas" (see Hasnes, "Preface," 9-11).

Certainly this story is not one of the best of the Father Brown tales. But it has its thematic interests, as well as others. Perhaps the best way to approach it is by noting that though G.K.C. wrote religious nonfiction, such as *Orthodoxy* and *The Everlasting Man*, he was also very much concerned with social problems, advocating Distributism, which was neither capitalism nor communism, and producing such volumes as *What's Wrong with the World?* and *Eugenics and Other Evils*. Since the comments about modern banking and economics are put into Father Brown's mouth, and since Father Brown is Chesterton's moral norm in these chronicles of corruption, this story should not be considered one with a religious point, but rather one moralizing upon institutional economic policies.

Two further introductory points need to be made before Father Brown's comments are considered. The first is simply that no comparison to Chesterton's other social writings is being made here. That is a worthy purpose, but it would be a far longer and different type of paper. This essay is merely a consideration of what a detective-story reader, if this tale had been published in, say, 1936, would have had suggested to him or her. Second, a slight part of the setting and narrative line must be given. This is intended simply for the orientation of readers to the context of the priest's remarks, and will not try to recapture the full complications of the story.

"The Mask of Midas" opens with Father Brown in the company of Colonel Grimes, a chief constable of a county, and Inspector Beltane, one of the men under Colonel Grimes. What county is never said, but the use of *county* could imply that the setting is Ireland, not England, where the word would be *shire*. Since southern Ireland has been independent since 1921 and since one character refers to the "British Constitution" (15), this would have to be northern Ireland. But English colloquial usage is not this precise in the distinction between *shire* and *county*, and none of the characters uses an Irish brogue—so probably Chesterton meant the setting to be an "industrial seaport" (13), with nearby moors (18), in England—probably but not certainly in England. In the opening, Colonel Grimes speaks at some length with Denis Hara, an American gangster, who presumably (the story does not say) has gotten into Great Britain because of his Irish ancestry—or possibly his Irish birth. If the setting were northern Ireland, this would have extra interest; as it is, Hara mainly introduces the possibility of criminal gangs into the story. At any rate, the precise setting, although interesting, does not seem to be necessary to the economic theme.

The three protagonists go to see "Sir Archer Anderson, the famous financial writer and organiser, . . . the head of . . . many . . . highly respectable banking enterprises" (16); he is in the office of the Casterville and County Bank, having recently come from London to check on the local banking affairs (15-16). The story is not ever clear, but probably he has set up independent private banks in various places, of which this is one; *Casterville* seems to be an invented name. Since Sir Archer seems to live in London, it seems odd (at least to a foreign reader) that he is a magistrate (16)—also called a J. P. (15)—that is, a Justice of the Peace—who can sign a search warrant for the county constabulary; but, upon request, this is what he does (19). Again, this Londoner being a magistrate is not significant to the economic theme.

One other background element needs to be introduced. Part of the discussion in the first part of the story involves a "convict [who] escaped" on the previous day from a nearby "large penal settlement on the moors" (18). "He is quite a poor man, accused of being a poacher . . . and there is no doubt that he killed a gamekeeper" (18). However, he received a short sentence because, in the circumstances, his act was more like manslaughter than murder (18, 23). At any rate, he did not stay to complete his sentence.

At this point, speeches by Father Brown may be introduced. The first is the longest:

> ". . . I am out of my depth. . . . Oh, I know well enough when I'm out of my depth; and I knew I should be, when I found we were hunting a fraudulent financier instead of an ordinary human murderer. You see, I don't quite know how I came to take a hand originally in this sort of detective business; but almost all my experience was with ordinary human murderers. Now murder's almost always human and personal; but modern theft has been allowed to become quite impersonal. It isn't only secret;

> it's anonymous; almost avowedly anonymous. Even if you die, you may catch a glimpse of the face of the man who stabbed you. My first case was just a small private affair about a man's head being cut off and another head put on instead [he is referring to "The Secret Garden," the second story in *The Innocence of Father Brown*]; I wish I were back among quiet homely little idylls like that. I wasn't out of my depth with them." (22)

If the 1936 mystery reader, who has been posited, knew the earlier Father Brown stories, what would he or she think? Two things, probably. First, that Father Brown was not perfectly accurate. He had dealt with modern financiers before. One example is "The Crime of the Communist" in *The Scandal of Father Brown*, where the priest solved the murder of two financiers—a Jew and an American, as they are identified—who were killed by a believer in economic Darwinism. It is true that the financiers were the victims here, but even so Father Brown comments, "Their views on economics and ethics were heathen and heartless" (tenth paragraph from the end). Thus, the reader of "The Mask of Midas" would be suspicious that Chesterton had some point he wanted to make, in Father Brown's protestation, at the cost of a slight inaccuracy.

Second, the reader might remember the introduction to *The Secret of Father Brown;* there Father Brown explains how he investigates a crime: he identifies the criminal by identifying with the criminal. Here is the basic passage:

> "I had planned out each of the crimes very carefully. . . . I had thought out exactly how a thing like that could be done, and in what style or state of mind a man could really do it. And when I was quite sure that I felt exactly like the murderer myself, of course I knew who he was." ("The Secret of Father Brown".)

What this implies is that Father Brown, the moral norm, cannot identify with financiers. Also by implication, it may suggest to the reader that he or she at least *should* not be identifying with them, either.

Why Father Brown cannot identify with them is not so

certain. Surely it is not because the desire for wealth and the power or the pleasure that wealth brings is so unusual as a motive. Money, after all, is the motive for many murders. Rather, it seems to be that it is hard to find a single person behind modern financial crimes; it is hard to be certain how many or who is responsible. Father Brown continues his discussion with a reference to the beheading of his "first" case as a "very individual incident"—by *individual* he seems to mean *personal,* but *individual* also carries the suggestion that there is one individual behind the crime. (There is also the repetition of *"in*dividual *in*cident" to recommend the phrasing.) Father Brown goes on:

> "Not like all this irresponsible officialdom in finance. They can't cut off heads as they cut off hot water, by the decision of a Board or a Committee; but they can cut off dues or dividends in that way. Or again, although two heads could be put on one man, we all know that one man hasn't really got two heads. But one firm can have two heads; or two faces, or half-a-hundred faces. No, I wish you could lead me back to my murderous poacher and my murdered gamekeeper. I should understand all about them. . . . " (22)

One notices in passing the parallelism of "my . . . poacher and my . . . gamekeeper" with the polyptoton of *murderous* and *murdered.* But the point seems to be the difficulty to attributing blame in an institution. Slightly later, Father Brown, in an anaphora ending with a polyptoton to another character's comment, says, "The bank next door is beyond my imagination" (23). No doubt this is hyperbole, but it conveys the same idea of an inability to identify with banking criminals.

One more of the same sort of comment may be quoted. This is in reply to a comment about the poacher, saying his punishment was reduced due to an "Unwritten Law" about the circumstances of the murder. Father Brown picks up on the phrase, using it perhaps to mean *morality,* and replies:

> "Modern murder still, very often, has some remote and perverted connection with an unwritten law. But modern robbery takes the form of littering the world with paper and parchment, covered merely with written lawlessness." (23)

Again, one notices in passing that the two clauses of this comment end with a polyptoton: "unwritten law" and "written lawlessness," respectively. But the point is that the alliterative phrase of "paper and parchment" suggests an impersonal relationship between the robber and his victim or, more likely, victims. It seems odd that Father Brown never makes a contrast between, say, the eighteenth-century highwayman, whose robbery victims at least saw him, even if he was wearing a mask, and modern robbery victims, who sometimes—or *often,* these statements suggest—do not know whom to blame.

Obviously, Chesterton is developing at least a partial truth here. In the present, when banks and savings-and-loans collapse after having been looted, probably by absentee owners; when sometimes banks are established primarily to be conduits of drug money and other financial chicanery; when (a few years ago) junk bonds were issued with the assistance of sometimes unnamed financial advisers to enable one company to take over another in a leveraged buyout, one cannot deny a certain social and moral truth to Father Brown's observations.

What follows in "The Mask of Midas" does not live up to this opening, unfortunately. That is, it turns into a usual detective story, with a number of reversals and surprises for the characters and (certainly in intention) for the reader. The single financier who has been introduced—Sir Archer Anderson—seems to be by himself responsible for whatever financial skullduggery has been done. The faceless robbers, uncertain in number, have here a face, a number—and a name.

It is true that Chesterton tries to retain the facelessness of this financier in a late speech by another character, after

Father Brown has said that Sir Archer certainly had not had his fingerprints taken:

> "The truth is," (says this other character), "that nobody seems to know very much about him; prints or anything else. When I started studying his ways, I had to start with a blank map that only afterwards turned into a labyrinth. I do happen to know something about such labyrinths; but this was more labyrinthine than the others." (32)

This does not sound typical of most modern bankers, not even those connected with such third-world affairs as the Bank of Credit and Commerce International (for a current example, from the news). It sounds more like a con man than a banker. But in 1936 it may not have seemed so strange; there was still a large amount of privacy for the wealthy, particularly in a reticent society such as Britain's. The modern electronic civilization has less privacy or more openness, depending on one's point of view.

There is only one other quotation that fits this pattern. Father Brown comments about the financier and the Irish-American gangster:

> "[Sir Archer] may have had dealings with Hara, neither perhaps telling the whole truth; such compromises are common in America between the big business man and the racketeer; because they are both really in the same business." (32)

Again, there is a partial truth here. If one thinks of the 1930s, with the gangsters in America making large amounts of money from illegal liquor during Prohibition and some of the attempts at union-busting on the part of some large businesses, one can see resemblances. Selectively, one can find parallels today: the use of kickbacks in some areas of the construction industry, for example, is much like the protection racket. Thus, both big business and the criminal gangs are, to some degree, "in the same business"; no doubt they sometimes have dealings with each other.

What conclusions can be drawn from Chesterton's story? The most obvious, in this context, is that G.K.C.

was able to use his fiction to make comments about the social world. Of course, one of these comments is about America, and it is always safer to moralize about foreigners than about fellow citizens—but that is only one comment out of a number aimed at financiers generally.

It is probable that Chesterton's choice of a priest as his detective allowed him greater freedom to moralize than would other choices. The priest is a better choice as a moral norm, a symbol (if one will) for truth. Certainly, Chesterton used Father Brown more than he did Mr. Pond and his other detective characters. And it is also true that Sherlock Holmes, Dr. Gideon Fell, and Hercule Poirot are not known for their denunciations of a corrupt society, and obviously not for religious comments such as Father Brown makes elsewhere—although Dr. Fell occasionally denounces modern literature.

Can one claim that anything is especially Christian about this story, other than Father Brown being a Christian priest? The answer is both yes and no. There is no overt Christian statement—no Biblical citations, for example. But Christians have had mixed relationships with the wealthy through history. It was the founder of the faith, after all, who said that it was as difficult for a wealthy man to get into Heaven as for a camel—or a rope, as some scholars would have it—to get through the eye of a needle. And, a bit later, it was the treasurer of the group around him who betrayed that founder to the cross. Perhaps there is reason for Father Brown to be suspicious of financiers.

If one is a reader of modern detective fiction, he or she will note also that modern detectives, however much they reach conclusions about human nature, seldom generalize about the corruption of financial managers, stockbrokers, or bankers as a class. Indeed, it is a likely guess that the editors of most journals would cut such comments, if they did not reject a story for containing them. Detective novels have more freedom, but it is seldom used. (Julian Symons, who had a reputation as a poet and a critic before he started writing mysteries, in the social themes of a number of his novels is one of the exceptions.) If nothing else, "A Mask of Midas" reflects an age not with greater opinions but with more freedom for expressing them.

Finally, one may conclude that Chesterton, like C. S. Lewis after him, used popular-literature forms to say what he wished to convey to a mass audience. In this case, the mystery reader of 1936, if he or she read with any sort of attention, would learn to beware of bankers.

Acknowledgment

John Peterson, whose "Father Brown Bibliography" has been cited, in a letter of 28 September 1991 critiqued an earlier version of this essay. The author thanks him for catching a problem in the discussion of the setting.

Works Cited

Chesterton, G. K. *The Mask of Midas*. With a Father Brown bibliography by John Peterson. Edited and with a Preface by Geir Hasnes. Illustrated by Noralf Husby. Trondheim, Norway: Classica forlag, 1991. 1–62 pp.

Hasnes, Geir. "Preface." Chesterton 7–12.

Peterson, John. "A Father Brown Bibliography." Chesterton 39–62. *Note:* This bibliography consists of three parts: Part one: The Father Brown stories in chronological order, 39–43; Part two: G. K. Chesterton on the mystery writer's art, 45–48; Part three: Father Brown Criticism and Discussion [the shift to capitals is in the original], 49–62.

The Exit of Father Brown

Ola Strøm

Chesterton, G. K.: *The Mask of Midas* / with a Father Brown bibliography by John Peterson; edited and with a preface by Geir Hasnes; illustrated by Noralf Husby. — Trondheim: Classica, 1991. - 64 p.: ill.

So the ultimate Father Brown mystery is a mystery no more. The last of the legendary unpublished manuscripts by Chesterton has seen print, and this world event has unexpectedly taken place in Norway. The print run being 1,000 copies at 350.—or 200.— Norwegian kroner depending on binding (equivalent to about $53.50 and $30.50), at last the most inveterate Father Brown completists should be able to read a story that till now has had a very limited circulation in manuscript copies.

Chesterton contemplated a new series of Father Brown stories in the middle 1930s, of which "The Vampire of the Village" was to be the first, and "The Mask of Midas" the second. For unclear reasons only these two stories were realised (as far as we know today) for although the preface of the book reviewed speculates on the existence of further Chesterton stories in obscure little magazines, I have a feeling that this is the end.

I should have been happy to tell you that the story was worth waiting for. The publisher thinks so, as he in an interview presents the story as not Chesterton's best, but neither his worst. Howsoever, I must disagree—it is probably the palest Father Brown story in print. The preface refers to a legend of the existence of a Father Brown story so lacking in quality that it was rejected by a potential publisher—a fact suppressed from Chesterton by his secretary—and calls this rumour improbable.

We will never know the information exchanged by Chesterton and his employee, but the literary facts stand for themselves: A publisher expecting to be offered a Father Brown story of reasonable vintage would be liable to question the merits of "The Mask of Midas." The fall-off even from "Vampire" is remarkable. Father Brown stories were admittedly in demand at the time, but a printing of this one would do no service to the author's reputation, as a conscientious publisher would be aware of. However, I feel none too certain that this story was ever offered to anyone.

The story is about an escaped convict and a bank manager who may be a criminal, and one should not give more away. The story has a beginning and an end, but no middle part. When you expect a development section, the unravelling has already started. Now, this is not unusual in Chesterton's oeuvre, where reality may well be brought forth from illusions without explicit detection. That is why many of Chesterton's plots are presented retrospectively through storytellers. This time, however, we are present at the moment of detection, and Father Brown reconstructs a complicated story by the mere fact that a man is too calm—a long and impossible shot indeed.

Like Ellery Queen (dying messages) and Erle Stanley Gardner (switched guns), Chesterton has his specialty: identity problems. This turns out to be the foundation of "Midas," but he did also use this gimmick as recently as "Vampire" and is by now repeating himself. In addition, parts of the plot border on the ridiculous, which could kill any story, but is fatal in a mystery story.

The figure of Father Brown has lost much life-blood and draws on routine. For all practical purposes, he is present in name only, and his name might well be substituted with that of another Chesterton detective without anyone noticing the difference.

Chesterton's preceding and last story collection was *The Paradoxes of Mr. Pond* (1937), with its retrospectives ("The Three Horsemen of the Apocalypse"), its detections ("Pond the Pantaloon"), and its simple paradoxes ("When Doctors Agree"). It also illustrates the possibilities of failure: "The Terrible Troubadour" is Chesterton's "Creeping Man"-allusion and a preposterous story, not due to what happens in the story but to what does not happen. But it shows how Chesterton even at this late stage turned a plot with insufficient possibilities for detection into a retrospective—just what he did not do with "Midas."

What do these points add up to? Contrary to the publisher of "Midas," I can understand why this story was suppressed and a new series killed, whoever was responsible. To be honest, I have difficulties accepting "Midas" as a finished product; it rather resembles a sketch covering possibilities (premises) of a plot, to be further developed and corrected. Being curious of its contents myself, I do not blame those responsible for printing the story, but I feel sad that the exit of Father Brown is so wanting in inspiration and execution.

As additional material, the book contains an interesting preface by collector and Chesterton bibliographer Geir Hasnes, and extensive bibliographic material on Father Brown and Chesterton's writings on mystery fiction by John Peterson.

Oh, yes, the address of the publisher: Classica forlag, Ragnhilds gt 10, N-7030 Trondheim, Norway. You might give it a try now that you are warned—if you are as curious as yours truly . . .   ◆

The Short Stop

Marvin Lachman

The Best Short Stories of 1991

Though, to the best of my knowledge, I read all the mystery short stories published in 1991, I was surprised at the limited number of sources for my non-baker's dozen of the year's best. Seldom has *Ellery Queen's Mystery Magazine* so dominated my annual list, garnering nine places. Its brother publication, *Alfred Hitchcock's Mystery Magazine,* seems to be in a slump and has very few major mystery writers in its pages. Having the big names, as EQMM does, is no guarantee of short-story excellence, but, on the other hand, there usually are good reasons why certain writers achieve fame. *Playboy* was the only other magazine to provide a story for my list.

1991 was a year of many good original anthologies, though *Sisters in Crime 4* was easily the best, and supplied the other two stories for my list. Here they are, the best of 1991, in order of preference:

1. Carolyn Wheat "Life, for Short" (SIC 4)—A harrowing story, with a hospital setting, of a terminally ill cancer patient, betrayed by "her Judas body." Clearly a crime story but one which also breaks your heart and stimulates your mind with its metaphors of life and death.

2. **Edward D. Hoch** "The Problem of the Country Church" (EQMM August 1991)—The best pure detective story of the year, with Dr. Sam Hawthorne called upon to solve the disappearance of an infant awaiting christening.

3. **Lucius Shepard** "Sports in America" (*Playboy* July 1991)—What starts as a routine mob slaying turns into a highly unusual story, with offbeat characters and biting dialogue. Here are more excellent metaphors, illustrating the love-hate relations the characters have with the sports teams of the Boston area.

4. **Linda Grant** "Last Rites" (SIC 4)—As Catherine Sayler helps an aunt, confined to a retirement home with a broken hip, solve a murder, she learns about mortality and aging.

5. **James Powell** "Santa's Way" (EQMM Mid-December 1991)—In the most unusual story of the year, the murder of Mr. Claus is solved, and a delightfully cynical attitude toward Christmas is displayed.

6. **Joyce Porter** "But Once a Year . . . Thank God" (EQMM Mid-December 1991)—Another Christmas story— and just as cynical, with witty dialogue and well-done detection.

7. **Donald Olson** "The Bigamist" (EQMM June 1991) —A long-time reliable contributor to EQMM (since 1969) outdoes himself with a variation on the old Alec Guinness movie, *The Captain's Paradise.*

8. **Virginia Layefsky** "This Place Belongs to You" (EQMM January 1991)—In her first story in EQMM in thirty years, Layefsky uses a fascinating, offbeat narrative style to tell about a lonely woman.

9. **Edward D. Hoch** "The Theft of Leopold's Badge" (EQMM March 1991)—The only repeater on this year's list combines two series characters, Captain Leopold and Nick Velvet in a story, with many twists, of murder, arson, and robbery at a museum. Included in the "cast" is Velvet's *bête noire,* the White Queen.

10. Doug Allyn "Sleeper" (EQMM May 1991)—A fine, hard-boiled regional mystery about Detroit, a city blessed in recent years by some very good writing from William X. Kienzle, Loren D. Estleman, Rob Kantner, and Allyn.

11. Clark Howard "Dark Conception" (EQMM October 1991)—A short novel which blends "science" with the author's well-known social consciousness and tops it off with the year's most suspenseful action.

12. Celia Fremlin "Yellow Ken" (EQMM January 1991)—A suspenseful story, also about aging, and a sick man's efforts to make his life meaningful.

Since my last column, many additional books of short stories have come my way, including, appropriately enough, Mr. Hoch's *The Year's Best Mystery and Suspense Stories 1991* (Walker, hardcover, $19.95), his annual anthology of the best stories of the previous year, 1990. This is one of his stronger collections, with two highlights, both about New York City. Stanley Cohen's "Hello, My Name Is Irving Wasserman!" is a most imaginative story about body disposal in the city. Carolyn Wheat's "Three-Time Loser" is an insightful picture of its criminal-justice system.

I'm opposed to anthologies restricted to authors of only one sex. Still, I'm always looking for a good story, so I've read all of the *Sisters in Crime* anthologies edited by Marilyn Wallace. As my selections above indicate, I thought SIC 4 (1991; Berkley paperback original, $4.99) was very good. In addition to containing two of my four favorite 1991 stories, there were very worthwhile stories by Karen McQuillan, Sharyn McCrumb, and Barbara D'Amato. This anthology may well be the mystery bargain of the year.

Also restricted to women and including five of the same authors as SIC 4, *A Woman's Eye,* edited by Sara Paretsky

(1991; Delacorte hardcover, $19.00), was a disappointing collection, with only stories by Nancy Pickard, Amanda Cross, and Liza Cody offering much. Pickard beautifully presents an unusual background, New Zealand, in "The Scar." Cross's strength is in presenting a professor entangled in the New York City criminal-justice system. Of the many social-problem stories in this book, Cody's tale of a homeless young woman is best.

Not finding as much to recommend in the stories as I would have liked, I found other things in the book. Paretsky's introduction succinctly and intelligently places the role of female mystery writers in perspective. It also contains avoidable mistakes, referring to Dorothy Uhnak's sleuth as "Christy Oper" and describing her as a New York Transit Authority police officer. The fictional detective's name was "Opara," and she was assigned to the District Attorney's office. It was *Uhnak* who was a former transit cop. Despite what the dust jacket says, at least one of the stories is not "new." I recognized Faye Kellerman's "Discards" from the November 1990 issue of EQMM.

I also note that, apparently, such is Sara Paretsky's clout, she was able to remove the ubiquitous Martin H. Greenberg from the cover and title page, something other anthologists like Hoch, Breen, and Pronzini have not done. Yet Greenberg, who does the important job of obtaining rights and permissions, is listed as sharing the copyright with Paretsky. Did someone feel an anthology of stories by women should not include a guy named "Martin" on the dust jacket?

A recent trend in mystery publishing is the recurring anthology. Besides Hoch's annual collection, there is *Sisters in Crime,* and the *New Crimes* series, edited by Maxim Jakubowski. The first of what is promised to be an annual collection of *noir* crime fiction is *Dark Crimes, Great* Noir *Fiction,* edited by Ed Gorman (1991; Carroll & Graf hardcover, $21.95). It includes nineteen short stories, two of which (by Gorman and Bill Pronzini) are new. There are also reprints of two out-of-print novels, Gil Brewer's *The Red Scarf* (1958) and Peter Rabe's *Anatomy of a Killer* (1960). Outstanding is Pronzini's introduction to the former, a model of what happens when someone who is knowledgeable and enthusiastic writes with compassion about a forgotten writer. The introduction by Gorman and Bill Crider to the Rabe book is quite good, too.

Though most of the stories and books I've written about up to here deal with social problems and fit into the category many consider "hard-boiled," lovers of the classic British mystery were not ignored in 1991. *A Classic English Crime,* edited by Tim Heald, was published in England in 1990 to celebrate the Agatha Christie Centenary and reprinted in the U. S. in 1991 by Mysterious Press, hardcover $16.95. There are twelve stories, mostly parodies and pastiches of Christie's work. There is also Simon Brett's mock scholarly essay regarding Poirot's origins. It's an enjoyable collection, though one best read in short doses.

Another anniversary, the 60th since the founding of William Collins & Sons Crime Club in 1930, was celebrated by another anthology. Apparently *A Suit of Diamonds* (1991; Dell paperback, $4.50) edited itself, because, though there are author introductions, no editor is listed. None of the stories is outstanding; those by Robert Barnard, Elizabeth Ferrars, and Sarah Caudwell are best. Still, I find the idea behind Caudwell's androgynous sleuth, Prof. Hilary Tamar, very gimmicky. Why is she withholding the sex of her series character?

Christmas Stalkings (1991; Mysterious Press hardcover, $17.95) was "collected by" Charlotte MacLeod. (Does that mean she did not edit it?) It is her second anthology of Yuletide mysteries. Six of the authors are the same as in *A Suit of Diamonds.* Again, we have an enjoyable group of stories, though there is nothing here to move either heart or mind. *Warning:* At least half of the stories, despite what it says on the dust jacket, are not about murder. Bah, humbug!

Three good anthologies were culled from our dwindling mystery-magazine market. *Scarlet Letters,* edited by the late Eleanor Sullivan (1991; Carroll & Graf hardcover, $18.95), consists of sixteen stories from EQMM, all having to do with adultery. *Home Sweet Homicide,* edited by Cathleen Jordan (1991; Walker hardcover, $18.95), has twelve stories, all relatively recent, from AHMM. Finally, there is another anthology which is part of that new growth industry, books with holiday mysteries. It is *Mystery for Halloween,* edited by Cynthia Mason (Signet paperback original, $4.99), with sixteen stories from those two magazines.

Though 1991 was not a great year for single-author collections, there were a few good ones to note. Max Allan Collins's *Dying in the Post-War World* (1991; Foul Play Press hardcover, $19.95) has five Nate Heller stories, all combining nostalgia and narrative quality. One even uses the case of William Heirens, who gained fame by scribbling on the wall after one of his Chicago killings: "Stop me before I kill again!"

The Night My Friend by Edward D. Hoch is a 1992 trade paperback (price not available) from Ohio University Press, Athens, Ohio. Edited by Francis M. Nevins, Jr., it continues the "Mystery Maker" series started at Southern Illinois University with collections of stories by Boucher, Fredric Brown, and others. This book has twenty-two nonseries stories, from the 1960s, by the Guest of Honor at 1991's Bouchercon, and they are ideal for readers who only know Hoch for his series detectives and impossible crimes. They demonstrate clearly what a reader-friendly writer Hoch is, someone who effortlessly draws the reader into the story, compelling him or her to stay with it to the end. There are ironic twists in many of these tales and, surprisingly, even some interesting philosophy to flesh out the characters. To cite only one example, in "Twilight Thunder" we enter a veteran's mind and read, "War is never won by men who do nothing, but Dale thought that perhaps peace was won that way."

I'm glad the interest in Margery Allingham's Albert Campion due to the television series *Mystery!* has reawakened interest in her books. Avon has reprinted a 1939 collection, *Mr. Campion and Others* ($3.95), and it is a joy to see how the author combined sophistication, character, and detection, all in short-story length. Three of the stories —"The Longer View," "Safe as Houses," and "A Matter of Form"—are outstanding, but several others among the thirteen stories are almost as good.

One of the most interesting (and worthwhile) projects in the field of the short story comes from Pulphouse. In addition to mainstream and science fiction, they have launched a regular series of paperback mystery short stories under their Mystery Scene Press. The Author's Choice Monthly line consists of collections, all priced at $4.95. Thus far we have *Deceptions* by Marcia Muller (seven stories, including a Western mystery); *Stacked Deck* by Bill Pronzini (seven stories, including a Nameless Christmas tale); and *Opening Shots* by Stuart M. Kaminsky, twelve items, including a short play, two Toby Peters stories, and one with Harry S Truman as detective. All collections include interesting introductions by the authors, written for this series. Future collections promise the work of Gores, Gorman, Garfield, Lutz, Estleman, and Block.

Also from Mystery Scene Press is a series of "Short Story Paperbacks," priced at $1.95 and beautifully produced; each contains one or two stories. The first five books are Edward D. Hoch's spy story, "The People of the Peacock"; Loren D. Estleman's prize-winning "Eight Mile and Dequindre"; two stories by Margaret Maron, one "Lieutenant Harald and the Treasure Island Treasure," about her series character, and another, "My Mother, My Daughter, Me," exploring relationships; two Nameless stories by Bill Pronzini: "Cat's-Paw" and "Incident in a Neighborhood Tavern"; and John Lutz's Edgar-winning Arlo Nudger story, "Ride the Lightning." Future authors in this series will be Pickard, Gorman, Max Allan Collins, Teri White, Crider, Yarbro, Howard Browne, McCrumb, Elizabeth Peters, and Paretsky.

These are series for collecting, as well as reading, and some of the Mystery Scene books are available in cloth or leather and in signed editions. For information, write to Pulphouse Publishing, Inc., Box 1227, Eugene, OR 97440.

Crime Novelists As Writers of Children's Fiction
VIII. Dorothy L. Sayers

William A.S. Sarjeant

Dorothy L. Sayers, 1944. *Even the Parrot. Exemplary Conversations for Enlightened Children.* Illustrated by Sillince. London: Methuen, vii + 55 p.

Dorothy Leigh Sayers had, by today's standards, a relatively short life, being only sixty-four when she died in 1957; but it was a life packed with industry, writing, and scholarship. The detective novels for which she was most famous, their hero Lord Peter Wimsey a dream of acumen and erudition, were only a small part of an *oeuvre* which included plays for stage and radio, verse, philosophical and religious writings, the editing of anthologies of poetry and crime fiction, translations from Dante and from such mediaeval works as *The Song of Roland*[1] and Thomas the Troubadour's *Tristan in Brittany*. The memorial plaque to

---

[1] Michele Slung notes correctly (*in* J. M. Reilly, ed., 1980, *Crime and Mystery Writers*, London: Macmillan, p. 1301-1304) that this was published by Penguin Books in 1957, but she does not note that it was read excellently by Anthony Quayle for a two-record album published by Caedmon—a recording highly recommended to anyone interested in Sayers' scholarship.

her in Somerville College, Oxford, was properly a tribute to a most distinguished scholar, as well as to a most memorable and individual writer.

Some of her minor works have been borne away to near oblivion on the torrent of her writings. Among them is the single work for children here considered; or was it indeed written for children? From format and illustration, one would say "Yes"; but its dry humour is likelier, one feels, to appeal to an adult audience. Only a child as "enlightened" (or perhaps one might better say, as precociously erudite) as the young Wimsey is likely to enjoy it. Ordinary children of the Second World War period would find its topical allusions comprehensible but the style difficult and much of the content entirely bewildering.

It is indeed written as a conscious and witty pastiche of the instructional works that must so have burdened the lives, and depressed the spirits, of the middle- and upper-class children of Victorian times. It features Nurse Nature and the two children in her charge, Matilda and Archibald Lively. Their conversations, albeit surely without resemblance to reality at any time in history, have many counterparts in nineteenth-century literature.[1] However, Sayers' versions are not so solidly indigestible; instead, they are an entertaining parody. Here is an example from the beginning (pp. 1-2) of "The Canary," the first of the five fables contained in this little book. The topic being discussed is whether the blackout, then imposed throughout Britain as a precaution against bombing raids, was beneficial or otherwise.

---

[1] A painless means for travelling this literary wasteland is to read E. M. Delafield's *Ladies and Gentlemen in Victorian Fiction* (New York and London: Harper and Brothers, 1937, 2974 pp.) Examples are to be found on p. 31 from Charlotte M. Yonge's *More Bywords,* 1890; on pp. 55-57 from the same author's *Hopes and Fears,* 1860; on pp. 36-42, and written earlier still, from Mrs. Sherwood's quite dreadful work *The History of the Fairchild Family,* pt. I, 1818.

"I think it gave our kind Mamma some little uneasiness," observed Matilda, "for Mrs. Airie was continually telling her that it was unwholesome to sleep behind those heavy curtains. But Mamma always replied that Papa knew best, in spite of old Doctor Draught, who shakes his head sadly and says that nobody can rest well without abundance of fresh air."

"And do you find, Miss Matilda, that you sleep worse since the windows have been blacked out?" inquired Nurse Nature.

"On the contrary, I sleep longer and more soundly—except, of course, when I am disturbed in the night by the siren. The thick curtains make the room quite dark all the year round, in spite of British Double Summer Time (which differs by two hours from Greenwich Mean Time and by sixty minutes from the old Summer Time we had before the War from April to September and now have for twelve months in the year)."

"That is quite right, dear Miss Matilda," interposed the Nurse, "but you should not make your informatory parentheses quite so long—you see, you are already breathless."

"That is a bad habit of mine, which I shall endeavour to correct," admitted Matilda.

As will be seen from the above, Matilda personifies the sort of child, having an enquiring mind but consistently obedient and imbued with sound religious principles, that a Victorian parent was expected to consider most desirable and praiseworthy. The resultant humour is sometimes rather wry, as is shown in the continuation of the preceding discussion (pp. 6-7):

"Dear me!" exclaimed Matilda, "how grateful we should be to Herr Hitler for imposing this excellent rule upon us, and thus improving our health and comfort."

"It is not reasonable, Miss Matilda," said the good Nurse, "to thank anybody for *imposing* upon you measures which you might have learnt from *me* and

> obeyed without compulsion. If the person to whom you allude has done you any benefit, it is not by his own intention, and gratitude is therefore misplaced. And besides, the title *Herr* should be reserved for gentlemen."
>
> Matilda was silent under this rebuke. . . .

Archibald is the naughty one, always necessary in Victorian writings as counterpoint to the virtue of another, usually elder, child. However, unlike his earlier counterparts, Archibald is not always left altogether convinced by his nurse's remonstrations! He is occasionally quite as reflective as his sister. When, in the fourth fable, the eating habits of "The Boa Constrictor" are being outlined by Uncle Peregrine to the children and their nurse, Archibald's comment leads to a response from Matilda that must have awoken echoes in many a woman's heart (p. 34):

> "Dear me!" exclaimed Archibald, "what a pity that human beings are not constructed on the plan of the Boa-Constrictor! Think what trouble it would save if we could consume all our rations for the month at a single repast! There would then be no necessity for this perpetual preparation of breakfast, luncheon, tea and dinner, all this setting and clearing of tables, and this washing-up of china and cutlery which absorb the greater part of the day for so many people."
>
> "Why, no," agreed Matilda. "If that were the case, there would be less reason to say that *a woman's work is never done,* and the females of every class would have far more leisure to employ in agreeable and intellectual pursuits than they have at present."

Though circumstances have changed since the 1940s, women readers will surely still relish the ruthless analysis of feminine abilities and male inabilities contained in the second fable, "The Bee-Hive." Archibald is again reflective (pp. 22–23):

". . . Besides," he added, plucking up his courage, "if there were no men, how would there be any civilization? For all the ladies would be occupied with bringing up their children, and would have no time, I am sure, for inventing machines and navigating the ocean, and delving in mines, and doing the hundred-and-one other things needful for our well-being and security."

"You can answer that question for yourself, Master Archibald," retorted his Nurse a little tartly. "How is this matter arranged, pray, among the bees of whom you think so highly? The workers there are all females, who by a suitable provision of nature, have been relieved from household cares, and have both leisure and strength to perform all the tasks for which their civilization calls, such as gathering the food, manufacturing the wax, building the cells and attending to the nurture and education of the young grubs. And you may see to-day that women are becoming more and more capable of taking over the work commonly assigned to the men, and doing it very well too. Nor does their comparatively feeble physique incapacitate them for these unusual exertions, since machinery driven by electrical power makes it possible for a single person to do, with the pressure of a finger, what in former days would have demanded the brute muscular force of many hundreds of strong men."

"That is true," said Archibald, stoutly, "but it was the men who invented the machines."

"And well they might," replied Nurse Nature, "for if they did not justify their existence by making some useful contribution to society, there would be a very good argument for condemning them to the fate of the drones."

"All the same," interposed Matilda, "they are surely very shortsighted; for each new invention that economizes power and labour makes it easier for the women to step into their place. When they have invented *everything* needful for the easy functioning of society, they will have outlived their usefulness."

The second fable, "The Cat," entertainingly treats with the changing relationships of children to their parents. Matilda's percipient comments involve Mother Nature in some embarrassed circumlocutions (p. 12):

> ". . . But surely, if the task of bringing up only *two* children is so very difficult, that of bringing up five, or nine, or even sixteen—which was the number of Great-Grandmamma Lively's family—must be harder still. Pray, what is the reason for that *decline in the birthrate* which was the subject of a leading article in yesterday's journal? Has the task grown so much heavier since our grandparents were children? Or must we think that our dear parents are less energetic and devoted than those of an earlier generation?"
>
> "The latter, I am sure, is not the case," said Nurse Nature with some haste and a considerable emphasis (for she desired her young people to think well of their Papa and Mamma). "It would be true to say that your parents are *more* devoted, and work much harder for your benefit than your remoter ancestors did for *their* children. I knew your Great-Grandmamma very well, and she was quite content to leave the upbringing of her offspring to me and to the two nurse-maids; we seldom saw her, indeed, in the nursery, except as a rare and honoured visitor; while an encounter with your Great-Grandpapa was, for the children, a truly awful occasion. Thus, your respected Great-Grandmamma was able to devote time and energies to the bringing of children into the world, which would otherwise have been expended upon looking after them."

The Second World War allusions, though recurrent, are sufficiently minor to present few difficulties to modern readers. In the last fable, "The Rabbit," the overlooking from a hilltop of a town that has been bombed not only leads on both to amusing comments but should also cause some uneasy reflections upon contemporary attitudes to architecture and town planning. The other participants in this conversation are Matilda's friend Angelina Wishwell and castle caretaker Mr. Ramrod (p. 50):

> "Why, of course!" cried Matilda. "We could bestow our cities underground. That would be easy enough, now that scientific discoveries and modern engineering have discovered the way to ventilate subterranean structures and to render them secure from collapse."
> "Why," exclaimed Angelina with distaste, "would you turn us all into a race of cave-men or *Troglodytes?* We have progressed further, I hope, than to imitate that kind of primitive and brutish people."
> "Pray, Miss," replied Nurse Nature, tartly, "where did you learn to speak with such contempt of your ancestors? The Troglodytes were respectable people enough, with refinement and leisure sufficient to cultivate the art of mural painting to a degree, and in a style, beside which the decorations of a modern tea-house or cinematograph palace appear both childish and vulgar. . . ."
> "But it would be very nasty and unhealthy," objected Archibald, "to live underground all day and never see the sun."
> "Yet Master Rabbit is stout and vigorous enough," replied his Nurse, "and displays no lack of cheerfulness in his behaviour."
> "I have thought of that," put in Matilda eagerly. "In my underground city there should be public lifts [elevators] at every convenient corner, so that people could come quickly up to the surface, which would be laid out in the prettiest pleasure-grounds imaginable. Think how delightful it would be, at the end of a morning's work, to emerge in a few seconds' time into beautiful gardens or the countryside, with no confined streets or dirty smoke to disfigure the face of Nature! And on their half-holidays, or at the week-end, the workers would not have to spend long hours in trains and omnibuses, or in a long stream of vehicles, in order to obtain fresh air

and green fields, for these good things would be waiting for them on their very roof-tops."

"Why, that's true," said Mr. Ramrod. "And think of all the good agricultural land that would be saved from being built over."

"And would you have nothing on the surface at all," said Angelina, "except fields and cows and forests and all that kind of thing?"

"Oh, yes," said Matilda. "I would have some beautiful buildings and fine old examples of architecture, which people could visit for pleasure; but I would put underground all the ugly factories and all the stores of food, and everything that could be of vital importance in time of war. And all the essential traffic should be hidden away as well, to leave the roads free for people who wished to travel agreeably and enjoy the landscape. . . ."

Have we missed an opportunity, in the years since the Second World War? Are we unnecessarily turning our world into a wasteland of concrete and asphalt? Perhaps, after all, we might have done better to imitate the rabbits!

This, then, is a delightfully entertaining book, should you happen on a copy; and Sillince's drawings add a subtle extra humour to the text. Did Dorothy Sayers truly intend it for children? Perhaps; but the book she wrote turned into one for adults. As a writer for children, then, I must deem that she failed. Instead, however, she produced five delightfully light-hearted fables for adults that deserve to be brought back into print, even fifty years later. ♦

The Greatest Misogynist of Them All

Maryell Cleary

From what I know of little Dimple, it would have been just like her to keep him sweating until the last minute. . . .'

"'You know your women, Chief,' Roden said dryly."

This is a typical comment from the books of A(lbert) B(enjamin) Cunningham (1888-1962), starring Sheriff Jess Roden of Deer Lick, Kentucky. These twenty-one mysteries, published between 1939 and 1952, show a leading character who is alternately attracted to and repelled by women. Women in the series are consistently flawed. Some are evil; others carry basically good impulses like mother love to extremes, with sad consequences; some are good but weak, needing male support; others are good but fail to understand their men. Most are mercenary and uncaring.

Jess Roden is a country sheriff from the little community of Deer Lick on the Green River. He lives in a cabin near the river, his companions his dogs. They are faithful and have no interest in money—much better than women! The dogs often play a role in the mysteries. Though some names and breeds change, some are consistent through most of the books. Big Boy is a favorite, tall as a calf, protective, and quite capable of knocking a man down and holding him captive. Carlo, the big red bird dog, is also generally on hand. Lead, the bony-tailed coon hound, earns his keep and more when there's a trail to be followed by smell alone. In some books there are others, such as Ace, the airedale, vicious on command, and Speed, the shepherd, who attacks first when he thinks there is danger. Except for the one book set in Texas, the dogs are present throughout, if only to welcome Jess home after a hard day.

The sheriff's other loyal companion is Big Nig, the big black riverman. He's always ready to take Roden up, down, or across the river, even when it's swollen by flood waters. He's a good man to have around when there may be a fight, or when errands need to be run. He will go anywhere with or for Roden, make himself a temporary home in some rough shelter, and do anything Roden needs done. He is utterly loyal and unquestioning, again in contrast to a woman.

Most of the time Roden is happy living on his own, keeping his simple home, fishing, hunting, working. Yet every now and then he is sorely tempted by a beautiful and seemingly competent woman, and falls in love. In one book he finds that the woman he's attracted to is actually the murderer he's seeking. In at least two others he finds a woman who appears to be just right and courts her. In each case she lets him down, mainly by not being willing to share his time and attention with his job.

In *Death of a Bullionaire,* Molly Weldon could have married Jess if she'd been more understanding. She likes him, is sexually attracted to him, and enjoys basking in his reflected glory. He is being honored in Texas, and she likes being associated with so renowned a man, but she can't understand that the renown depends on undivided time and attention given to his cases. It's great watching him beat the local target-shooting champion, but when Roden asks her a question about the case rather than the romantic question she's expecting, she flings herself out of the car, angry. She's jealous of the women he meets in his job, though she has no reason to be. When he misses a date because the case is breaking, she goes off to the movies with another man and refuses to listen to Jess's explanation. And this is the best of the women!

Roden's—or is it Cunningham's?—attitude toward women is delineated in *The Death of a Worldly Woman*, when the author writes about the women of Norton, the city in which the murder occurred:

> The women of Norton were roughly classified into four groups. There were the conventional housewives—women who prepared breakfast, got their children off to school, and then spent the better part of the morning piddling around the house, sometimes dressing and going out to do a bit of shopping, but often remaining in robes and mules till around noon. Some enjoyed living, but most of them were sullen, railing at their husbands for not taking them out more, hungering for the hot spots. By the rank and file of Norton these women were referred to as stick-in-the-muds. They lived, but not excitingly; they functioned, but with no glamour; things happened to them, but not interesting things. In Norton's opinion they were relics—of a distant time before people had learned how to live.
>
> There was a second group, composed mainly of widows living snugly on insurance left to them by husbands who had worked themselves to death while their wives idled or played contract bridge or sipped tea from fragile cups. These women were usually old and not a little pathetic. Had they been men they would have formed a club, or used a barbershop or the bar or the park benches, where they would have played checkers and told smutty stories and had a good time generally. But being women and too contrary to get along together, they were for the most part solitary—going to the movies or out for Sunday dinner at the Norton Inn or on a shopping tour and bringing back gadgets such as ash trays that could be clipped to bridge tables. But mostly they just sat around. Norton referred to them indifferently as has-beens.
>
> The third group was made up of ambitious young things married and unmarried; conceited and designing, deliberately childless if married, and not too innocent of the facts of life if unmarried—young matrons and maids saturated with the Hollywood ideal; reading the charm and movie magazines; preening themselves in the hope of catching the eye of a talent scout, their hair properly coifed and their eyebrows plucked and their mouths made up in a kissable pout. They had not got anywhere yet, but

> they were on the way and they knew exactly where they were going, which was in the direction of the Sophisticates.
>
> Dimple Guest had been a Sophisticate. Small and blond and richly gowned, her golden slippers had peeped from the interior of rich limousines onto the carpet which led to every hot spot in Norton. And inside, her sables thrown back, she had dined and danced. At the crowded soirées she had moved richly and confidently, her poise unshakable.

This passage capsulizes the author's attitude toward women. Though I have only three of the books on hand right now, I have read enough of the others to know that this is not just a fictional account of the women in one fictional city. In book after book, women are portrayed as basically, perhaps biologically, flawed. They flirt and attract men by their sexual wiles, then are faithless. What they want most from men is money, whether simply for security or for social prestige, furs and jewels, comfortable homes, and the "hot spots." Of Dimple Guest, Roden said, "She was marryin' another meal ticket." In his view, that's what most of them were out for.

After marriage they are likely to ignore their husbands and focus all their love on their children. Often they spoil their offspring, particularly sons, and favor them over anyone else. In *Death Haunts the Dark Lane* Clara Groat marries a rich widower with two children, pretending that she loves the children and will be a good mother for them. In fact, she hates them because they will inherit rich farms from their mother's estate. She does her best to put them down and push her own son forward. That they are good-looking and capable while he is not does not raise them in her estimation. When the elder, Gay, is killed on reaching her majority, Clara is a natural suspect. In *Death of a Worldly Woman* another doting mother tries hard to throw suspicion on everyone else but her son, who was the murdered woman's fiancé.

Good women in these books are few. Some are colorless or victims, needing men to support and protect them and give their lives meaning. Fay Mankin, in *Death of a Worldly Woman,* lives a drab, gray life, always fearful of being molested by her uncle, until she falls in love and the love is reciprocated. Then her personality comes to life. In *Death Haunts the Dark Lane* the best woman is the murder victim, killed before the reader can even meet her. In *Death of a Bullionaire* the murdered man's widow seems to be a basically good person, but her husband is old and she falls in love with his handsome son, making herself a prime suspect in the case.

When Molly has hung up on him, at the close of *Death of a Bullionaire,* Roden says to his friend, "It hurts, Chief. It hurts more than anything I ever came up against." He goes on, "Who was that old feller that said priests and soldiers should stay single? The idea was that without a woman to distract 'em they'd be free to put their whole mind on their work." After which Roden takes a plane back to Kentucky, the river, the dogs, and Big Nig. One gets the feeling he won't let himself fall in love again.

Today we might call Roden and his creator "male chauvinist pigs," but this seems to go deeper than the conventional chauvinist attitudes toward women. It makes me wonder about Cunningham's personal life, his experience with women, and what hurts he might have had as a child and an adult. One does not get so completely cynical and negative about half the human race without some good reason. Since he's not around to ask, we'll have to let this go. But, readers, be forewarned: Jess Roden may be the greatest misogynist mystery fiction has ever seen! ♦

The Backward Reviewer

William F. Deeck

James Corbett. *Murder While You Wait.* **U.K.: Herbert Jenkins, 1937, 311 pages.**

Readers—oh, all right, one to be exact, and she was pixilated—have insisted that I at least occasionally remind them of the works of James Corbett, that unfortunately neglected genius of the thriller. Since this is the final issue of TMF and thus vociferous complaints from others cannot be published, I will courageously risk it.

If you are unacquainted with his works, the first thing to be said about Corbett is that when the familiar disclaimer is printed—"All the characters in this novel are purely imaginary and have no relation whatsoever to any person, living or dead"—he is one of the very few authors telling the literal truth. Or one certainly hopes he is.

In this novel, Reginald Harcourt, M.P. for West Singleton, has been shot down in front of his residence after receiving a threat from "Murder While You Wait," or M.W.Y.W. Seth Mannering, a rich barrister who had talked with Harcourt the night before his death and scoffed at the death threat, hires Malcolm Egerton, distinguished criminologist, to investigate the case. It is a complicated one, for twenty-six other people are apparently also in danger.

Harcourt and the others had testified in the Broxton Financial Scandal. Some of the group begin receiving notices of their imminent death, and die they do. One is stabbed to death in a taxi, while another is murdered by machine-gun. When one of the threatened men commits suicide, Egerton explains it this way: "He was bluffing in Daly's Café, *and he left a note to that effect!*" (The emphasis is Corbett's.) Since you are all experienced and perceptive readers, you will understand that without my having to explain it.

One person is threatened by M.W.Y.W. and is surrounded by Egerton, Mannering, the heroine, and a Scotland Yard detective. He dies anyhow at precisely the time predicted after having a nip of brandy. Mystery buffs will immediately suspect one of those four individuals. But if they do they will have forgotten that this is a James Corbett novel; the man actually died of a heart attack, a pure, if that's the word I want, coincidence.

Several times it is pointed out by the investigators that if they knew the name of the killer, they would have a better chance to catch him. As his many admiring readers are aware, Corbett never spares the logic.

When another stabbing death occurs, Egerton keenly orders an X ray. That, he is sure, will reveal that the same knife was used in the two murders. Unfortunately, the reader is never vouchsafed the results of this forensic miracle.

Near the end of the novel, Egerton reveals the reason for his superb investigative ability: "I always get into contact with the unseen, with the mystic forces of the universe, then, after a long period of waiting, there comes a light in the picture." Some readers, unused to Corbett's characters, might wonder why he didn't get in touch with the unseen earlier to solve the case; others might wonder why he isn't doing it even as he speaks. Actually, since he is a Corbett character, he never does it.

Or maybe he did and he doesn't reveal it. He catches the murderer by identifying the five distinct clicks from a call-box when the killer picks up the receiver. Since the murderer hadn't at that point given Egerton's number, perhaps mystic forces did after all put a light in the picture.

John M. Eshleman. *The Long Window*. U.S.: Ives Washburn, 1953; Mercury Mystery No. 206, n.d., 126 pages, as *Death of a Cheat*.
_____. *The Long Chase*. U.S.: Ives Washburn, 1954; Mercury Mystery No. 201, n.d., 126 pages with a two-page introduction by Anthony Boucher, as *The Deadly Chase*.

When Lucy Storm is found strangled in her bedroom after a party in *The Long Window*, Police Lieutenant Larry Koharik of an anonymous city next to Berkeley, Calif., directs the investigation. Since the partygoers have alibis, the obvious suspects are the husband, who may have killed her because of jealousy, and the black houseboy, who apparently was angry with her for disrupting his plans to return to school. Despite the fact that Koharik once dated Lucy and knows at least one of the suspects, he continues as head of the investigation. Don't policemen ever recuse themselves when there might be a conflict of interest, or is that fit only for judges and potential jurors and some lawyers?

While not a great deal is learned about Koharik of a personal nature—quite often in first-person narration these details aren't provided—it is revealed that he is thirty-three years old and married to a woman who loves, and thus puts up with, him.

Though the investigation is a bit unorthodox, with Koharik socializing with the people who partied at Lucy Storm's house, it is a good one. Oh, there's at least one hole in the explanation, the murderer oddly is quite bloodthirsty and then reluctant to kill, and a suspect hides where he and Koharik had been just a few days before. But none of that is noticed in the reading, for the author carries all before him with splendid prose, solid suspects, and an attractive protagonist.

In addition, not that anything extra was needed, there's a great bit about lie detectors when all the suspects—but you should read it for yourselves.

In *The Long Chase,* Koharik and his wife are at a society party, meet the rich and noble Señor Diego Castillo, furnish him with a ride, and watch him be shot for the third and fatal time. Then Koharik discovers that Castillo was neither rich nor noble and had a fair number of enemies.

Let me step aside here for a moment and quote a master reviewer, Anthony Boucher, from his introduction to this novel:

> Koharik is clearly destined for a niche of his own among the very few sympathetic and believable cops of tough-realistic fiction. And he has a worthy case to work on in this book—a case that involves criminal factors (gambling, pandering) that might happen anywhere, and social factors that could happen only in the American West, from the peculiarly Californian meaning of being a daughter of the Dons to the unique practices (as sincerely devout as they seem anti-social) of schismatic Mormons exiled from Utah as heretics. It's a case that builds, like good Hammett, out of quiet personal tension into violent overt action, culminating in an outburst of wholesale carnage which is as underplayed and as effective as anything in that line since *Red Harvest.*

Boucher goes on to hope that there would be more cases for Lieutenant Koharik. Unfortunately, there were no others. Thus we will be vouchsafed no additional observations from Koharik such as the following:

> Talking to the chief is something that sends goose pimples up and down his back. I think the reason he's a captain is because the chief knows it and likes it that way. There are never any arguments from that kind of captain if you're a chief. The reason I'm

a lieutenant is because that kind of captain needs somebody around who can do the work that he can't.

For reasons only a publisher would understand—I sure don't—Mercury Publications chose to publish Eshleman's second novel featuring Lieutenant Koharik before it published the first one.

J. H. Wallis. *Murder by Formula.* U.S.: Dutton, 1931; U.K.: Jarrolds, 1932, 286 pages.

During a meeting of the elite Aristoi Club, the Hanging Committee—art, let me hasten to say—discusses crime novels. Several members urge Andrew Wingdon, best-selling author who writes, according to one character, "readin' books," to write his own detective novel, or "trash" book. The formula proposed to Wingdon, as he iterates it:

> Story gripping, distracting, entertaining, but not grief-producing—no reality of death; a murder early in the book—first or second chapter, followed by at least one more to prevent loss of interest; the murdered a person or persons of consequence in the story, . . . continual atmosphere of menace to principal surviving characters, . . . no wholesale murders, no use of madmen, animals or artificially bred humans; the guilty always in full view and prominent; the detective supplied no more information than the reader; London and Scotland Yard or Manhattan and the New York police; and a beautiful girl wooed and won by the end of the story.

Wingdon begins making notes and the others depart. The next morning Wingdon is found dead in the club, killed more or less in the manner discussed the previous evening.

At the end of his novel, Wallis claims in verse that he himself followed the formula. For the most part I agree with his contention, particularly since fair play was not a criterion.

The investigation by Inspector Jacks, in the first of several novels featuring his alleged abilities, is slipshod or negligent. For example, Jacks is unaware that apartments and houses have rear entrances and that a murderer might use them. A locked-room murder occurs that is given no thought by Jacks and is explained in one unlikely sentence during a most unlikely dénouement. Jacks gives Wingdon's widow, with whom he is smitten—see the last sentence in the formula—an automatic to protect herself at a meeting she shouldn't attend but provides no instruction about use of the weapon, though this may be excused, I suppose, because the automatic turns out to be a revolver.

Maybe in his later novels Wallis either is more careful with his plot or writes more persuasively. Maybe.

Dorothy Gardiner. *The Seventh Mourner.* U.S.: Doubleday, 1958; Popular Library, 1964, 128 pages, as *The 7th Mourner;* U.K.: Hammond, 1960.

Sheriff Moss Magill, of Notlaw, Colo., population 415 counting two unborn babies and home of the third worst hotel in the country, is left $100,000 in the will of a late citizen of Notlaw—though her death does not seem to deplete the population—if he will escort her ashes to Scotland and bury them on top of a mountain. For reasons not made clear, Magill is not interested in the money and does not want to go to Scotland. However, the stipulations in the will lead him to believe, again for reasons not made clear, that one or more of the legatees might be murdered if he doesn't.

Magill is an engaging character and worth meeting despite his not preventing murder. In addition, Gardiner presents the Scottish Highlands lovingly. But more should have been done with Magill's culture shock, and the mystery aspect undoubtedly could have been handled better. For example, the villains are obvious and witless. Enjoy

Magill and the scenery and try not to pay too much attention to the plot.

Robert Sidney Bowen. *Make Mine Murder.* **U.S.: Crown, 1946; Black Knight No. 30, n.d., 168 pages.**

Gerry Barnes—recently of the OSS, and another fine illustration of how we won the war despite dreadful incompetence—has opened his own private-eye office. Independently wealthy, all he lacks is a customer. He tells one of his girlfriends that he won't marry her, but if she can get him a murder case he will let her help him crack it. A few minutes later she calls to report a murdered man in her apartment. As Barnes is about to leave his office, he is more or less kidnapped by a potential client who wants him to find a man about whom nothing is known.

Try as I might, I can find no satisfactory explanation why this novel was published even once.

Dougal McLeish. *The Traitor Game.* **U.S.: Houghton Mifflin, 1968; Popular Library, n.d., 158 pages.**

What connection is there between John Lane's being sent to jail for a crime he didn't commit and the assassination of the Canadian Prime Minister? Very little, I have to report. Nonetheless, Lane, upon his release from prison, becomes involved with his friend Max Gervais in trying to stop the violent breakup of Canada. Of course, he doesn't know that is what he is doing until the villain, another unfortunate criminal mastermind let down by his minions although he, too, blunders, reveals all in this thriller.

Elsewhere I have reviewed McLeish's *The Valentine Victim,* his only other crime novel. It, too, is set in Canada, but the flavor of the country is missing. In *The Traitor Game* we learn a lot more about Canada, particularly its politics, and apparently not much in this area has changed since the book was published. Yet of the two books I preferred *The Valentine Victim,* a first-class fairplay police procedural, though both are very well written.

Admirers of Jerome K. Jerome, of whom I hope there are many, will be incensed at one point in this novel when one of the heroes attributes a Jerome quotation to Hillaire Belloc.

Alice MacGowan and Perry Newberry. *The Million-Dollar Suitcase.* **U.S.: Stokes, 1922; International Fiction Library, n.d., 326 pages; U.K.: Hutchinson, 1922.**

Impossible-crime fanciers get a bonus and a debit here. The bonus: There are two locked-room situations. The debit: They aren't very good.

The first occurs when a San Francisco bank teller absconds with nearly a million dollars. Close on the teller's heels is the bank's private detective, Jerry Boyne. He arrives at the teller's hotel room to find the windows latched with burglar-proof locks and the door closed with the usual spring lock. In front of the door is a woman repairing a rug, and she had been there since the teller had entered his room. The teller had not left by the door, but neither he nor the money was in the room.

Worth Gilbert, whose father has stock in the bank, offers the bank's board $800,000 for the contents of the suitcase. It seems he needs a challenge. While Gilbert can raise most of the money, he has to ask his father to provide the rest. After a fight with his father, he doesn't get the money. Shortly thereafter his father is found shot to death in the second locked room.

Fortunately for Boyne, who would not have been chosen by his predecessor to head the detective agency and one can see why from the many mistakes he makes in this investigation, he has the aid, on the rare occasions he's sensible enough to use it, of a young woman whose psychologist father trained her from childhood to be a lightning observer and reasoner. She figures out the first locked room; Boyne, after having the solution shoved under his nose, solves the second.

This novel apparently appeared first in the *Saturday Evening Post* as *Two and Two*. As far as I can recall, the *Post* printed no bad stories, but it did publish some mediocre material, in which category this falls, despite an occasional good observation such as "A financier's idea of indecency is something about money which hasn't formerly been done." Since this is the first in a series of books featuring Jerry Boyne, I'll be looking for the other novels by MacGowan and Newberry but only to establish who solves Boyne's other cases.

Wilson Tucker. *The Chinese Doll.* **U.S.: Rinehart, 1946; Detective Book Club, n.d., 158 pages; U.K.: Cassell, 1948.**

While you might think that a private detective in Boone, Illinois, would be underemployed, you would be right. In this documentary novel—in the form of letters from Charles Horne to Louise, the woman he is in love with—Horne is in his office trying to keep warm and working on his book, *Lost Atlantis,* of which seven chapters have been completed. Into the office comes Harry W. Evans, who gives Horne $500 to bail him out of jail since he claims he will inevitably be arrested for spitting on the sidewalk, or jaywalking, or shoplifting, or whatever.

Naturally, Horne is somewhat nonplussed, for the authorities in Boone are not noted for monkey business. To coin a phrase—or is it a clause?—little does he know. Evans leaves Horne's office, and as Horne is watching, a

Studebaker sedan with supercharger strikes Evans, killing him, and then speeds off. Later Horne is invited into another Studebaker with supercharger, this time a coupé, driven by a beautiful Chinese girl, and ends up at an illegal gambling club.

All of this and another "accidental" death tie in with Evans. Horne doggedly and intelligently—though not brilliantly—investigates, getting some idea of who Evans was through Evans's membership in an amateur publishing association and discovering another beautiful Chinese girl.

Even after he'd metaphorically rubbed my nose in it, Tucker fooled me on the villain, for which I give him great credit. The novel is well-written, amusing, and believable—up to the point of revealing the villain. While I probably won't make myself clear here, I accept that the villain was who Tucker says it was—the facts, once Horne pointed them out, prove it—but I don't accept that the villain was who Tucker says it was. You'll have to read the book to see what I mean, and you ought to read it anyhow for it's an excellent private-eye novel.

For more about Tucker's Charles Horne, see Len Moffatt's article in *The Mystery Fancier,* Vol. 12, No. 2.

G. V. Galwey. *The Lift and the Drop.* **U.K.: Bodley, 1948; Penguin Books, 1951, 221 pages.**

Since his theory of how to catch a murderer is examining the past of the victim, Chief Inspector "Daddy" Bourne has a real dilemma here. For there were six people in the lift at Pleydell House, home of *The Voice* and other publications, when it plummeted out of control from the sixth floor to the basement. If any of them were meant to die, which one was it? Or was it an act of mindless terrorism, since no murderer could be certain whom he or she might kill?

A bit too much emphasis on the technical aspects of the murder, a lot too much on the seafaring aspects—I got quite lost as soon as water was approached—a nebulous political scheme, and a murderer with more hubris than I could accept are the weak points here. The strong points are the characters of Bourne and Sergeant Griffiths and their investigation. Well worth reading, and a nimbler mind than mine might find my objections not significant.

Richard Burke. *Murder on High Heels.* **U.S.: Gateway, 1940; Arrow Mystery Library No. 5, n.d., 125 pages.**

Once the thrill, not likely to last even microseconds, has passed from the discovery that the detective's name is Genghis Donne—his brother's name is Kublai—which occurs on the second line of Page 1, there isn't much left of interest here. Since Clarence Elden, the murdered man, was president of the New York branch of the American Purity League, was owner of a sizable pornography collection, and apparently had a planned assignation with a female for purposes ostensibly impure, Burke could have had some fun with this situation. He doesn't.

Occasionally I am introduced by mystery authors to others as a "critic." I respond that actually I am a reviewer. Reviewers appraise, or try to appraise, as in my case, what the author has written; critics tend to deal with what the author would have written if the author had been only half as talented as the critic.

Thus, I am not going to criticize Burke for what he didn't do in his first novel. I shall merely say that what he did was create, or more accurately borrow, stock characters—among others the dumb and antagonistic cop, the dumb and friendly cop, and the show girl down on her luck—and a plot so forlorn that I kept reading only in the hope that something, anything, fresh might appear. My hope was dashed.

Constance and Gwenyth Little. *Great Black Kanba.* **U.S.: Doubleday, 1944, 188 pages; U.K.: Collins, 1945, as** *The Black Express.*

Of all the subgenres in crime fiction, amnesia is my least favorite. The Little sisters here have made me forget —unintentional and probably unfunny joke—that bias with a not too plausible but entertaining story of a young woman who loses her memory after a blow to the head while on an Australian train—called Great Black Kanba, or snake, by the aborigines—in the early days of World War II. Worse, the young woman's identity is mixed up with another female's, and she is laid claim to by an odd family containing a blackmailer and perhaps a murderer.

Apparently the different areas of Australia built different gauge railroad tracks. To travel through Australia meant getting off one train and on to another; each change creates problems for the protagonist. The young woman loses her memory on one train, and on two others some unfortunate people have their throats slit.

Good fun with a plucky heroine, but don't look for fair play.

Carolyn Wells. *The Moss Mystery.* **U.S.: Garden City Publishing, n.d., 119 pages, in** *Four in One Mysteries.*

"I am a living man, and he is a Fictional Detective, but that is the only way in which I radically differ from Sherlock Holmes. We are both wonderful detectives, and I know of no other in our class." Thus sayeth Owen Prall, who then goes on to add to the misquotation: "Elementary, really, my dear Watson."

Readers of my reviews are aware that I am easily taken in by specious authors, which Wells to her credit, even when she may be trying, generally isn't. As Prall is presented with the case he has desired his entire career—murder in a locked room—I was delighting in the spoof that Wells was engaged in as she made fun of her detective, whose ego is enormous. Reluctantly I was soon forced to conclude that Wells was serious in her intent, but this doesn't detract from the pleasure of reading this short novel as a parody. If you wish to read it for other reasons, so be it, but don't blame me if it is then far less enjoyable.

Jean Lilly. *Death Thumbs a Ride.* **U.S.: Dutton, 1940; Black Cat Detective Series No. 6, 1943, 128 pages.**

"Two murders would probably have gone unsuspected during the last year if Eunice Hale had not eaten a chicken croquette of questionable virtue." The two murders were the death of a woman, of apparently natural causes, at a tourist camp in the Adirondacks and the presumed hit-and-run death of a senator's gardener in the same area. Even with the aid of the chicken croquette they would have remained unsuspected except for the interest of vacationing district attorney Bruce Perkins, who is asked to investigate a jewel theft but prefers to find the alleged hit-and-run driver and begins to doubt the naturalness of the woman's death.

While the opening sentence is a good one, the rest of the prose does not get any better than slightly above pedestrian and the characters are essentially lifeless. Lilly somewhat makes up for this with her primary setting, unusual in mysteries, I believe: a lower-middle-class tourist camp. (Could there be such a thing as an upper-class tourist camp?)

Lilly also provides a, for the most part, fair-play mystery. For the most part, I say, since I could find no explanation—and I certainly couldn't figure out—how the gardener died, or even if it was murder. Maybe the Black Cat publication was abridged and the publisher neglected to mention it.

Leslie Ford. *Murder in the O.P.M.* **U.S.: Scribner, 1942; P. F. Collier, no date, 235 pages; U.K.: Collins, 1943, as** *The Priority Murder.*

Lawrason Hillyard seems to have the best of both worlds. He produces virtually the entire output of promethium, a highly sought metal needed to fight World War II; he also, as a one-dollar-a-year man, issues the priorities on it for the Office of Production Management in Washington, D.C. In addition, he is rich, he has enemies, he has a shrew for a wife, and his assistant is the young man he bribed to break off with his daughter when the young man was a nobody. Dead is how you expect Hillyard to end up, and you won't be disappointed, at least in this aspect of the novel.

While I generally enjoy Ford's nonseries novels and the books she wrote as David Frome, this is only the first of seven novels I have tried featuring Grace Latham and Col. John Primrose that I have been able to finish. This feat was managed by my holding grimly on to both covers, which made turning pages both a physical and a mental chore, since I knew if I put it down I would never pick it up again. It has the slickness, and particularly the depth, of a page in *The Saturday Evening Post,* where I believe it originally appeared.

There is nothing here to recommend. Even the setting—the nation's capital in wartime, which must have been a fascinating place—is given shoddy treatment on those occasions it's acknowledged. Moreover, the continuing conflict between Latham and Primrose, who address each other as Mrs. and Colonel and who want to get married but are not allowed to because of the objections of Primrose's man, Sergeant Buck, is nonsensical. One can understand Bertie Wooster's being dominated in this fashion by Jeeves, but Primrose is Buck's intellectual superior. Or is he?

Peter Hunt. *Murders at Scandal House.* U.S.: D. Appleton-Century, 1933; Dell Mapback No. 42, n.d., 239 pages.

In this, the first novel featuring Alan Miller, chief of police of Totten Ferry, Conn., when he isn't doing his various other jobs, Miller is on a vacation he feels he doesn't need and is definitely not enjoying the Adirondacks. Who could blame him if his description of the mosquitos, flies, and gnats is accurate? In fact, the mosquitos are the first murder weapon in the novel. Miller and a game warden check out some overactive buzzards and find a man tied to a tree, drained of blood and filled with poison by the mosquitos. This is a first in my reading of mysteries, and I hope it's a last. I can't think of many less pleasant ways to die.

The dead man was a chauffeur at the Balmoral Camp, inhabited by Lydia Whyte-Burrell, relict of the unlamented Edgar Burrell, infamous for his evil ways and his various byblows, some of Burrell's relatives, various hangers-on, and servants.

Though not a genuine detective, Miller is asked to investigate since the police are focusing on the more obvious but unlikely suspects. When asked how he is going to operate, Miller replies:

> Prowl a bit, and hope a great deal, and not ask too many questions. Murderers seldom tell the truth. The more clever questions I might ask, the less I would probably find out. If a man plans a killing, he plans an alibi and a reasonable accounting

of himself, and that sort of thing only confuses me. Besides, the duller I seem to be, the more careless the murderer will be. Therefore, I shan't be very bright. I'm not at all bright by nature, so it saves me a lot of effort. Now you know my method.

In a review of the second novel by Hunt, *Murder for Breakfast*, in another publication, I said that Miller, though out of his depth professionally—remember, he is only a part-time policeman—is nonetheless an intelligent man with a sense of humor. That is still true here in a not-strictly-fair-play novel.

For those who may be interested, Hunt was a combination of George Worthing Yates and Charles Hunt Marshall.

Lynton Lamb. *Death of a Dissenter.* **U.K.: Gollancz, 1969, 160 pages.**

Old Silas Finch doesn't like the church bells ringing in the English village of Fleury Feverel, or anything or anyone else for that matter. He defiles the cricket field, threatens his neighbors, lets the air out of bicycle tires, and is accused of molesting a quite molestable young woman. So it is nothing of a surprise that he ends up dead, but quite astonishing that he dies in the church ringing chamber, where someone has apparently bashed him in the head with a bench.

As the evidence accumulates, Detective Chief Superintendent Quill and Detective Inspector Bruce are somewhat dumbfounded to find that the facts point in only one direction: toward the rector of the parish, Frank Fenwick, an inveterate truth teller who says he didn't do it.

Fortunately for a U.S. reader, the cricketing is brief since, at least to me, it was quite incomprehensible. Also a problem is the local dialect, which is almost as impenetrable as the cricket and there's more of it. To make up for that there is a great deal of humor, some fine writing, a solid investigation, information on campanology, and an unusual solution, which I guess is possible. All in all, a nearly first-class first novel, particularly if you understand cricket and the local dialect.

By the way, could there really be such a thing as a Surveyor of Ecclesiastical Dilapidations?

Bill S. Ballinger. *The Tooth and the Nail.* **U.S.: Harper, 1955; Sherbourne Press, 1971, 243 pages, in** *A Bill S. Ballinger Triptych;* **U.K.: Reinhardt, 1955.**

A damsel in mild distress captures the attention of Lew Mountain, professional magician, and he comes gallantly to her rescue. She arrives in New York with a hatbox, an exceptionally heavy small satchel, and no dollar to pay the cab driver. Soon she joins Mountain's act and marries him.

Inevitably, given the folly of the female in distress, tragedy ensues. Mountain then—and I give away nothing here, repeating only what the author says in the prologue—avenges murder, commits murder, and is murdered in the attempt.

While I can't wax as enthusiastic as some reviewers have over this novel, it definitely is an enjoyable reading experience. ◆

It's About Crime

Marvin Lachman

Notes on Recent Reading

The recent death of Roy Fuller (see below), an author I had never read, led me to remedy that and read his best-known mystery, *The Second Curtain* (1953; reprinted by Academy Chicago, $4.95). It's a mystery in which literature is important to the story, as befits a work by one of England's most prolific and best-known poets of the post–World War II era. Its protagonist is George Garner, a marginal British novelist, whose prospects seem to be looking up. In addition to inheriting money, he is given the chance to edit, at a surprisingly good salary, a new literary magazine. However, his good fortunes seem tied to two mysterious deaths, which he reluctantly investigates. Garner tends to think of everything in literary terms, accepting personal praise as if it were a favorable review. Even his involvement in a crime is analogized to "the probable improbability of a Dickens novel." I found the end disappointing, though some who do not like books ending neatly may like its ambiguity. Fuller wrote well, and *The Second Curtain* is worthwhile reading for most of its way.

Fuller was no more literary-minded than Michael Innes, yet both his books and Innes's *Death on a Quiet Day* (1957; reprinted by Penguin in trade paperback, $8.00) are basically thrillers. Innes writes about David Henchman, a university student hiking in Devon, who discovers a corpse and finds himself living one of the busiest and most exciting days of anyone's life. Fortunately, Sir John Appleby is on hand. There is spying in addition to the murder, but it has a timeless quality, allowing one to enjoy it today, while so many of the novels with hammers and sickles on their cover are as hopelessly out of date as those with swastikas. Henchman dashes about in order not to become the next victim. (With great understatement, Innes has him think as he runs: ". . . there was much to be said for terror. It got you along.") There is also detection, but it is certainly not typical of the Golden Age between the world wars, though Innes is one of the few people alive today who was writing then, and he started with classical puzzles. There is an important literary clue, but it is almost impossible to guess, so one must conclude that although this is a good book, its strength does not lie in fair-play detection.

Charles Addams is arguably the mystery writers' cartoonist, for so many of his thirteen hundred cartoons, mostly published in *The New Yorker* from 1932 through 1990, dealt with crime. *The World of Chas Addams* (1991; Knopf hardcover, $30.00) seems destined to be the definitive Addams collection, containing his first cartoon as well as some which appeared posthumously after his 1988 death. It contains three hundred cartoons and twenty-four of his *New Yorker* covers. Almost every possible crime is included: murder, robbery, suicide, torture, etc. Two cartoons deal with Poe, and one contains a character who is very much a Father Brown lookalike. There is even one dealing with that delicious cliché of the Golden Age: murder in the snow, with no footprints left.

I was amazed at how many of the entries in Tony Thorne's *The Dictionary of Contemporary Slang* (1990; reprinted by Pantheon in trade paperback, $15.00) deal with crime. Besides the definitions that one expects in this sort of reference work, there is fascinating detail regarding the origins of the words. Among those you'll find are "rozzer," British slang for a police officer, and "shamus," with a lengthier than usual discussion of its argued-about origin. There is also a good discussion of variations of "nark," a British word so different from "narc."

In a recent issue of *Firsts,* Ellen Nehr discussed some of the unusual methods publishers used to sell mysteries during the Depression. We may only be in a Recession as I write this (January 1992), but there are signs publishers are going beyond normal promotion. Carroll & Graf, St. Martin's, and Mysterious Press are all holding contests for their hardcovers. Academy Chicago has revived the old Ace double mystery with a trade paperback edition of Elizabeth Sanxay Holding's *The Innocent Mrs. Duff* (1946) and *The Blank Wall* (1947) for $10. (Anyone wishing to chart inflation may remember that the original Ace doubles were first published in 1952 for 25 cents each. They were generally hard-boiled. However, a second set of Ace doubles was printed about a decade later, for 50 cents each, and six of those were devoted to Holding books, including the current two.)

The Innocent Mrs. Duff is suspected by her wealthy, far older husband of having an affair, and he sets about trying to frame her. *The Blank Wall* concerns a middle-aged housewife whose husband is overseas and whose teenage daughter has become involved with a married man. It was filmed by Max Ophuls, in 1949, as *The Reckless Moment* with Joan Bennett and James Mason. In both books deaths result from domestic conflict. It is good to see Holding, a writer much praised by Raymond Chandler and Anthony Boucher, back in print. She was one of the earliest (and best) writers of the psychological-suspense novel so popular in the 1940s. Behind her seemingly effortless prose style was considerable subtlety and shadings of character, especially in marital relations. This new "double" may become a collector's item, despite its rather uninspiring cover art.

I don't usually review guide books, but Don Herren's *The Dashiell Hammett Tour* (City Lights Bookstore, 261 Columbus Ave., San Francisco, CA 94133, trade paperback, $9.95) is a worthy exception. This is the first revision in about a decade of Herren's guide, and it is a significant improvement over the first edition. The heart of the book (85 pages) is a tour of the places Hammett lived in and wrote about. Twenty-nine locations are covered, and there are three very clear and useful maps and twenty-two photos, more than in the previous edition. However, the most significant improvement in the new guide is a greatly expanded, forty-page biography of Hammett, one which, despite all that has been written about him, still manages to make fascinating reading. For those who know Hammett's work and have been to San Francisco, it only takes the price of this book and some imagination to follow Sam Spade and the Continental Op (and Hammett) on their journeys up and down the hills of that city.

DOOM WITH A VIEW

I'm hard put to recall a better police procedural on television than *Prime Suspect,* shown on *Mystery!* in late January and early February 1992. Even *Hill Street Blues* pales somewhat in comparison. Perhaps it was seeing four hours of taut drama, *sans* commercial interruption. Helen Mirren's performance as a detective chief inspector assigned to her first big murder investigation, after years of sex discrimination, was outstanding, as good as anything I've seen in years. Her singleness of purpose, frustration, and fatigue were superbly conveyed. She headed a large cast, all of whom were believable and excellent. I love the "light" fare on *Mystery!*—Rumpole, Poirot, Campion, et al. — but *Prime Suspect* was meatier (and better) than usual.

The often surprising Public Broadcasting System, with a program called "The Golden Age of Television," is reviving shows from the fifties, and some are mysteries. Watching the first in the series, I was surprised to see the Charles Bronson of the early 1950s (after he changed his name from Buchowski) appearing in an episode of *Federal Men*, the syndication title for *Treasury Men in Action*, a series which ran from 1950 through 1955. Nostalgia buffs will enjoy shows like this despite its unsubtle dialogue, predictable ending, and primitive production values.

Considering the length of his career and his 85 films, Gary Cooper probably played in fewer mysteries than almost any other major star. *Operator 13* and *Cloak and Dagger* were about spying. *City Streets* was a gangster melodrama. *The Wreck of the Mary Deare* was an adventure thriller, based on a Hammond Innes novel, with an Eric Ambler screenplay. Not until his last film, *The Naked Edge* (1961), did an obviously ill Cooper play in a murder mystery. He starred opposite Deborah Kerr in an adaptation of Max Ehrlich's *First Train to Babylon* (1955). The movie, its setting transported from the U. S. to England, is about an American businessman (Coop) whose testimony results in the conviction of a fellow employee in the murder of their boss. The crux of the film is the growing suspicion on the part of his wife (Kerr) that it was *he* who committed the murder and a concurrent robbery of sixty thousand pounds from the firm. Good photography, with imaginative camera angles, helps the mounting suspense which, as the climax approaches, is considerable. Cooper and Kerr are quite good, as are the rest of a strong supporting cast, including Diane Cilento, Eric Portman, and Michael Wilding.

I've long appreciated the similarities between the Western and the mystery, with crime the common element in both. *The Films of Hopalong Cassidy* by Francis M. Nevins (a name not unknown in these pages) confirms that belief. This very large trade paperback, available for $19.95, from World of Yesterday Publications, Route 3 Box 263-H, Waynesville, NC 28786, is required reading for nostalgia buffs. It discusses the Hoppy movies and television shows and includes complete credits, providing some fascinating bits of information. For example, Lee J. Cobb appeared in them as Lee Colt in the late 1930s, and a young Robert Mitchum was in many of the Cassidy movies of the early 1940s. The book is handsomely illustrated, with more than three hundred film stills, reproduced with great clarity. Reading the plot descriptions shows that Hoppy does a great deal of detection, including following trails and figuring the trajectory of bullets. Now, if only someone would solve the legal problems and make these movies readily available again on television.

One staple of the "B's" was the Falcon series, and many of those films have been on American Movie Classics cable network. The script for the first Falcon movie, *The Gay Falcon* (1941), contains an example of that delightful small genre: mystery writers confusing anatomy, sometimes for humorous purposes. In this movie, screen writers Lynn Root and Frank Fenton have Wendy Barrie tell George Sanders (Gay Laurence, the Falcon), "I'm so scared I can feel my heart beating in my knees."

Death of a Mystery Writer

Henry Wilson Allen on Oct. 26, 1991, at age 79 (location not known). Under his pen names Will Henry and Clay Fisher, he was known for Westerns, though there were crime elements in books like *MacKenna's Gold* (1963), filmed with Gregory Peck, and *The Squaw Killer* (1968). He also wrote for television, including an episode called "A Mighty Big Bandit" on *Tales of Wells Fargo* in 1959.

Rudolph R. Caputo on Aug. 3, 1991, at age 77 (location not known). A member of MWA, he was the author of two books on police science: *Interrogation for Investigators* and *Criminal Interrogation*. He had been a special agent for the U. S. Treasury Department and U. S. Naval Intelligence. He also founded his own detective agency.

Theodore de la Torre-Bueno in 1991 (date and location unavailable) at age 76. He published his first mystery (the 600th first in EQMM) at age 68. The story, published in February 1983, was "Abduction into the Seraglio" and is a clever pastiche of the Dr. Samuel Johnson series, published in EQMM since 1943 by his sister, Lillian de la Torre.

Mel Dinelli on Nov. 28, 1991, at age 79, in Los Angeles. He wrote radio and television scripts and also had film credits, including *The Spiral Staircase* (1946) and *The Widow* (1949), based on a Cornell Woolrich story. His own short story, "The Man," achieved an unusual "hat trick," appearing in at least four media. This tale of a woman menaced by a psychotic itinerant handyman first appeared in *Story* magazine for May–June 1945. (It was reprinted in EQMM December 1953.) Dinelli adapted it for the famous radio program, *Suspense,* and also made a play out of it, one which opened on Broadway at the Fulton Theater on Jan. 19, 1950. Don Hammer played the title role; Dorothy Gish and Peggy Ann Garner also starred. Using a screenplay by Dinelli, it became the 1952 RKO movie, *Beware, My Lovely.* Ida Lupino played a young widow, and Robert Ryan was the handyman.

Roy Fuller on Sept. 27, 1991, at age 79, in London. In addition to being a corporate lawyer, he was one of the best-known poets in the English generation following W. H. Auden, publishing at least 38 volumes of verse. Despite his business career, he was also a deeply committed Marxist, though he renounced that ideology late in life. His mysteries have been called "moral thrillers," with the most famous being his first, *The Second Curtain* (1953), discussed above.

Ernest K. Gann on Dec. 19, 1991, at age 81, at San Juan Island, Washington. He was best known for adventure novels with aviation themes, including *The High and the Mighty, Fate Is the Hunter,* and *In the Company of Eagles.* One of his books, *Of Good and Evil* (1963), is listed in Hubin.

Howard Haycraft on Nov. 12, 1991, at age 86, in Hightstown, N. J. Most serious fans of the mystery who are age fifty or older probably first read *about* the mystery in one of Haycraft's two landmark books, *Murder for Pleasure* (1941) and *The Art of the Mystery Story* (1946), an anthology of articles by famous mystery writers and critics. With Frederic Dannay, he co-authored "The Haycraft-Queen Definitive Library of Detective Crime Mystery Fiction" (1951). He also edited anthologies of fiction and won two Edgars. Haycraft's father-in-law was the historical novelist, Thomas Costain, who in the 1940s wrote crime stories for EQMM under the pseudonym "Pat Hand."

Lenore Glen Offord on April 24, 1991, at age 85, in Ashland, Oregon. She wrote two series of mystery novels, one about Coco and Bill Hastings, the other about pulp mystery writer Todd MacKinnon. In addition, from 1950 until 1982 she was mystery critic for the *San Francisco Chronicle.* Her last book, *Walking Shadow* (1959), was set at the annual Oregon Shakespeare Festival in Ashland and used the experience of the Offords' daughter, Judith, who had worked in it as a student. Judith eventually became a choreographer for the festival, and in 1988 Offord moved to Ashland, after living in Berkeley, California, for fifty years.

Russell O'Neill on Dec. 18, 1991, at age 64, in New York City. He was a novelist and playwright whose work often was about crime. It included such novels as *The Alcatraz Incident* (1971) and *The Homecoming* (1980), and the play *Don't Call Back,* which was produced on Broadway in 1975 with Arlene Francis.

Gene Roddenberry in October 1991 in Los Angeles (other information not known). Though best known for *Star Trek,* the former Los Angeles police sergeant wrote for such shows as *Dragnet* and *Naked City.*

Douglas G. Shea on May 23, 1991, at age 81, in Philadelphia. His short story "Advice Unlimited" was published in EQMM December 1976, the 453rd "first story" to be published in that magazine. It was a humorous story with such characters as Inspector Attilan Hund and Gary Cooper Rabinowitz. He then became an active member of MWA.

Grace Zaring Stone on Sept. 29, 1991, at age 100, in Mystic, Connecticut. Hubin's Bibliography lists *Dear Deadly Cara* (1968), under her own name, and three books under her Ethel Vance pseudonym: *Escape* (1939), *Reprisal* (1942), and *The Secret Thread* (1948). *Escape,* an exciting novel of Nazi Germany, was filmed with Robert Taylor, Norma Shearer, and Conrad Veidt. Films were also made of two of her nonmysteries, *The Bitter Tea of General Yen,* starring Barbara Stanwyck, and *Winter Meeting,* with Bette Davis.

Jack Tannen on Dec. 10, 1991, at age 84, in Hollywood, Florida. With his former partner, Jack Biblo, for more than fifty years he operated Biblo and Tannen, one of the most famous book stores when Fourth Avenue near 14th Street was New York's leading area for books. They closed their business in 1979. Tannen wrote a book describing how to identify first editions. In the 1960s, Biblo and Tannen began publishing books, and one of their ventures was the reprinting, in 1968, of Haycraft's *Murder for Pleasure* (1941), then out of print.

Jean Francis Webb on Oct. 10, 1991, at age 81, in New York City. His very varied writing career began in the 1930s in the pulps. He wrote at least fifty mystery stories, but also wrote adventure, romance, and Westerns. His first novel was *No Match for Murder* (1942). Webb wrote many romances, including Gothics, under his own name, which he did not have to change because many readers thought the writer was female. He also wrote as Roberta Morrison. Two of his Gothics were set in Hawaii, and he wrote books on the history of those islands. With his wife, Nancy, he wrote the *Chick Carter, Boy Detective* radio series from 1943 to 1945. They also edited *Plots and Pans,* an MWA anthology of recipes.

Related Deaths

Dame Judith Anderson on Jan. 3, 1992, at age 93, in Santa Barbara, California. Considered one of the great actresses of the twentieth century, she was best known for her stage performances as Lady Macbeth and Medea. Her film career was less distinguished, but she did make some mysteries, including her role as Mrs. Danvers, the housekeeper, in *Rebecca* (1940). She also appeared in the title role of an embarrassingly bad film, *Lady Scarface* (1941), in *Laura* (1944), and in the first (and best) film version of the Agatha Christie classic, *And Then There Were None* (1945).

Ralph Bellamy on Nov. 29, 1991, at age 87, in Santa Monica, California. A versatile actor whose career spanned seven decades, he won his greatest renown for his portrayal of Franklin Delano Roosevelt in the play (and film) *Sunrise at Campobello.* He was known as the actor who perennially lost the leading lady in movies to more sophisticated actors, like Cary Grant in *His Girl Friday.* Bellamy appeared in many mysteries, including *Footsteps in the Dark* (1941) and *Lady on a Train* (1945). He also played Ellery Queen in four "B" movies at Columbia in 1940–41. On television, he was one of the first actors to play a private detective, portraying Mike Barnett on the successful series *Man*

Against Crime, beginning in 1949. Many years later, in 1970, he played Criminologist Ethan Arcane in *The Most Deadly Game,* a series which was unsuccessful, despite being based on a concept of Eric Ambler's.

Jose Ferrer on Jan. 19, 1992, at age 80, in Miami, Florida. He gained his greatest fame acting as Cyrano de Bergerac, Iago in *Othello,* and Barney Greenwald in the film version of *The Caine Mutiny.* Among his mystery roles were the 1949 film *Whirlpool; Orders to Kill* (1975), the original Kojak television pilot; and a 1973 television movie, *The Marcus Nelson Murders.*

Mame Fish on April 8, 1991, at age 79, in Fairfax, Virginia. The widow of mystery writer Robert L. Fish, she established a fund, after his death in 1981, for an award in his name for the best short story by a new writer.

Fred MacMurray on Nov. 5, 1991, at age 83, in Los Angeles. Although a generation remembers him only for his Disney comedy films and for his sitcom *My Three Sons,* which ran from 1960 to 1972, he made two noteworthy mystery films: *Above Suspicion* (1943), from the Helen MacInnes novel, and *Double Indemnity* (1944), the classic film *noir* from James M. Cain's novel. MacMurray played Walter Neff, the insurance agent who falls in love with Barbara Stanwyck, who wants him to help her kill her husband.

Daniel Mann on Nov. 11, 1991, at age 79 (location unknown). A famous television and film director, among his mystery films were *Our Man Flint* (1966), a spoof of the James Bond-type films, and *Willard* (1971), about an army of killer rats.

Yves Montand on Nov. 9, 1991, at age 70, in Senlis, near Paris. He was famous the world over for his acting, singing, and controversial politics. He probably first gained fame for *The Wages of Fear,* a suspense film by Henri-Georges Clouzot, based on the 1950 novel by George Arnaud. In it, Montand played a truck driver hauling a load of nitroglycerin over mountain roads in Central America.

Gene Tierney on Nov. 6, 1991, at age 70, in Houston. Her stunning good looks made her a popular movie actress, especially in the 1940s. She is still best known for playing the title role of the murder victim in *Laura* (1944), taken from the novel by Vera Caspary. Among her other mystery roles were *The Iron Curtain* (1948), as the wife of Igor Gouzenko, a Russian defector, in a movie based on a true spy story; *Night and the City* (1950), from Gerald Kersh's novel of London crime; *Where the Sidewalk Ends* (1950), based on William Stuart's *Night Cry;* and *Black Widow* (1954), from the Patrick Quentin novel. Tierney played Iris Duluth, wife of his series character, Peter Duluth. ♦

Verdicts

(Book Reviews)

Jill Churchill. *Grime and Punishment.* New York: Bantam, 1989. $3.50.

Whether or not you enjoy *Grime and Punishment* will probably depend on your tolerance of domestic trivia. In this paperback original, alibis depend on car pool and Little League schedules, and crucial evidence is deduced from PTA meetings and pot-luck dishes. Those whose lives are grounded in such suburban artifacts will better relate to this world than those more oriented to mean streets.

In a supposedly empty house, a cleaning lady is strangled with a vacuum-cleaner cord. But was she killed because of who she was, who she was thought to be, or what she knew? This is the puzzle Jane Jeffry, housewife and widowed mother of three, takes it upon herself to solve. Before the mystery is unraveled, surprising facts surface about Jane herself, her late husband, and their friends and neighbors. Below the surface idyll of this tranquil suburb, seething passions and dark secrets do indeed lurk.

The cast of more or less interchangeable suspects is largely female, with the exceptions of Jane's Chicago-policeman-friend-of-her-late-father's (shades of V. I. Warshawski) and the township detective on the case. (Ever since *Compromising Positions,* the housewife seemingly must be attracted to the cop.) Jane Jeffry is an appealing character, if a rather reluctant and accidental sleuth. However, like most housewives she could use an injection of self-esteem: everyone pushes her around, and she considers cleaning her son's hamster cage an assertion of her personality (don't ask). The publisher promises a series, with the next to be *A Farewell to Yarns.*

A small nit to pick: the cleverness of the title pun has been undermined by the cover designer, who used a fancy script for the first word which makes it read "Crime" instead of "Grime" at first glance. Incidentally, the author is in reality historical novelist Janice Young Brooks, writing under a pseudonym. It is hoped that in future mysteries she will use her strengths of clever plotting and well-written dialogue, and minimize the essentially mundane and repetitive details of domestic engineering. (Meredith Phillips)

Jo Bannister. *The Going Down of the Sun.* New York: Doubleday Crime Club, 1989. $12.95.

The Sun of the title is a yacht, the *Skara Sun,* which goes down in an explosion. The wife of a ruthless Scottish industrialist dies, but somehow her shipmate escapes with only minor injuries. He would have drowned, however, if he hadn't been resuscitated by Clio Marsh, a doctor-turned-mystery-writer who happens to be anchored nearby with her detective inspector husband.

It would help the reader to be familiar with the geography of the west coast of Scotland and with sailing terms and boats, as most of this book takes place on one boat or another. If there are any other books about Clio Marsh, it would also help to have read them, as many hints are dropped about her past and rather improbable career.

The survivor of the explosion, Alex Curragh, is a beneficiary of Alison McAllister's will, which incites her husband Frazer to a jealous rage. He storms into the hospital room, grabs Alex by his broken arm, and thunders, "Are you the wee shite that murdered my wife?" McAllister's vicious persecution, and that of his henchmen, provide the plot foundation for the rest of the story. There are so few suspects that the cause of Alison's death does not remain a mystery for long, so the second half of the book becomes a chase along the lochs and waterways.

Clio is a distinctive and original point-of-view character. Her personality is acerbic and somewhat abrasive, her reactions melodramatic. Her "world turned upside down" when she found a bit of evidence. She has the "unbelievably vile sensation" of being followed when a reporter simply wants to interview her. She says she's been kidnapped when Frazer invites her into his limo and drives around and around the car park. She finds a hunted man out of sheer intuition.

Balancing these overreactions are interesting perspectives and ruminations on nature and morality. However, it's hard to forgive her impetuosity and harebrained plotting resulting in an innocent man's death, and her casual dismissal of her responsibility. *The Going Down of the Sun* is definitely different, and a must for sailing or Scottish buffs. (Meredith Phillips)

Marcia Muller. *There's Something in a Sunday.* New York: Mysterious Press. $3.95.

Private investigator Sharon McCone's automobile-expense receipts must raise eyebrows at her employer's, All Souls Legal Cooperative in San Francisco. In *There's Something in a Sunday* she trails a suspect from a Lombard Street motel to Golden Gate Park to a coastside garden center to the Sunset District to Fishermen's Wharf—and that's only the Sunday. The rest of the book takes her into San Francisco's garment district and flower market to the Haight Ashbury to Hollister (100 miles south), back to Golden Gate Park several times, and back and forth across the city. Along the way we meet the widely varied denizens of these milieux, from the Park's homeless to the Hashbury's new yuppies.

One of Muller's main writing strengths has always been a strong sense of place, beautifully evoking and describing myriad aspects of the Bay Area. But this book takes in almost too wide a slice of northern California; the mixture is occasionally indigestible.

Sharon McCone's character, however, grows steadily more interesting and complex, and several of the other characters are keenly observed. For instance, when Vicki Cushman, the NIMBY activist, speaks, one can sense her insecurity and the source of her desperate and paranoid behavior:

> All these new things. New styles. Blush wine. The music—my kids play it. I don't even know who the singers are. Or why anyone would bother to listen to it. California cuisine. Is pasta salad still in, or has it gone out? Running? Eastern religions? The new sobriety—God, I just got used to cocaine. I don't know, I don't get out much anymore. At least not in what Gerry calls the right circles. And when we do, I don't know how to talk to these people. I mean, I'm trying to keep the corporations and that damned university from eating my neighborhood alive, and they're discussing exotic varieties of *lettuce,* for God's sake. Or is designer lettuce out too, now? Maybe that was last year. . . .

We also get glimpses into the lives of Sharon's colleagues, Hank and Rae; one of the pleasures of a series is continuing minor characters and how their lives impinge on the major one. The plot, as usual, is beguilingly tricky; the action will probably satisfy PI fans. But it has become Sharon McCone herself, "the mother of the woman PI," whose growing maturity and complexity keep us coming back for more. (Meredith Phillips)

M.R.D. Meek. *The Split Second.* **New York: Worldwide Library, 1989. $3.50.**

"[Lennox Kemp] had spent some six years in the wilderness, deprived—and quite justly—of the privilege of practising his profession, but now the Law Society in its wisdom had reopened its doors to him. . . ." Apparently the particulars which led to Kemp's disbarment and subsequent career as a detective are given in the first book in this series. The curiosity of readers who begin with the second, *The Split Second,* will be unsatisfied, for that is all the author has to say on the subject.

As a combined holiday and farewell assignment from McCready's Detective Agency, Kemp is asked by his employer's Scottish wife to investigate the disappearance of her niece. Fiona Davison-Maclean has vanished shortly after inheriting the substantial family estate from her domineering mother. A dowdy spinster, the heiress is now ripe for exploitation by any passing cad, her relatives fear.

Braving the Siberian rigors of Glasgow in February, Kemp traces Fiona's lighthearted and lightweight cousin, Lindsay, who has discovered the heiress's recent marriage to an opportunistic traveling salesman. But before the detective can find their island hideaway, Fiona drowns in the loch. The widower, Fergus O'Connell, consoles himself with an old girlfriend, hairdresser Lisa Ferguson, who shocks the village by moving in as "housekeeper."

Lindsay is furious that Fiona's holographic will, made the day of her death, leaves everything to her husband and nothing to her cousin. He's determined to pin the death on the "murdering bastard," in spite of Fergus's ironclad alibi, and sets out on a detective/spy mission. Kemp's attraction to Lindsay's "mistress" Alex, plus a subsequent death, keeps him on the case.

The cast of characters is so small that the reader trying to guess whodunit will be truly baffled. Author Meek (a retired woman lawyer living in England) ties up the plot strands adroitly in a completely surprising but fair-play conclusion. Her "talent to deceive" is equalled by her skill in nuance of characterization and poetic writing style. A minor quibble: too many character names beginning with the same letters, L and F: Lennox, Lexie, Lindsay, Lisa, Fergus, Ferguson, Fiona. The Scottish dialect is not overdone, and *The Split Second* beautifully evokes myriad aspects of Scotland, as well as entangling the reader in a most enjoyable web. (Meredith Phillips)

Sharon Singer Salinger. *Reckless Abandon.* **New York: Simon and Schuster, 1989. $17.95.**

Reckless Abandon is subtitled "A Novel of Mystery and Romance." Some mystery readers may find it too heavy on the latter, though modern-romance fans will probably lap it up. Several yuppie amateur sleuths eventually sort out two murders and quite a few miscellaneous crimes, more by bumbling around than by actual detection. The police and various federal agencies in this seaside town (which coast is never specified) are constantly ignored and hindered in their duties, for quite a few unconvincing reasons. The point-of-view character, artist Nell Styles, drifts into HIBK situations, and reasons more with her hormones than with her head.

In spite of the unlikely plot and general flakiness of the characters, though, *Reckless Abandon* is an enjoyable read. The writing is sensuous and evocative: food and wine, houses and landscapes, children and dogs all come to life in the reader's imagination. Motherhood and women's friendships are treated seriously. Humorous narrative and dialogue speed the book along.

The plot is so convoluted that it couldn't really be called fair play, though the publisher's blurb and author's acknowledgments do their best to give it away. The book is written in the present tense, which some readers dislike. On the whole, however, *Reckless Abandon* will probably appeal to the *thirtysomething* crowd. (Meredith Phillips)

Lindsey Davis. *Shadows in Bronze.* **New York: Crown Publishers, 1990. 342 pp. $19.00.**

Shadows in Bronze, the second book of the private-eye adventures of narrator Marcus Didius Falco is, like the first, witty, lively, well characterized in dialogue and action, a page turner. It dramatizes the public and private lives of first-century Rome. Falco is now an informer (not a spy, he insists) for the Emperor Vespasian. This position might give Falco a chance to raise his social rank—if he ever manages to get enough sesterces to invest in land.

The novel opens with his assignment to dispose of a corpse. It's an assignment far more nauseous than lucrative, but for Falco the beginning of looking for political intrigue. Six parts move rapidly from late spring AD 71 to August, and from Rome to southern Italy, to the Bay of Neapolis, and back to Rome. Dramatis Personae and maps are again provided, and a fan (who could be anything else after reading the first book?) relishes encounters with Helena Justina, whom Falco thinks of no longer seeing, with his long-time friend Petronius of the Aventine watch, and with other remembered characters. New are Falco's appealing 14-year-old nephew Larius, the sacred goat Falco acquires before the amazing horse, Little Sweetheart.

Falco admits to being "an outspoken, introverted rough neck" (p. 37), but a reader knows he is much more than that: sensitive, honest, intelligent, shrewd and capable, even if he does not like the sea and cannot swim. In addition to political intrigue, here is the intrigue of getting a reader to live with Falco and the sounds, smells, goods, clothing and distinctive people of Imperial Rome. Again—Ave, Falco! A rave review of a compelling read. (Jane Gottschalk)

Gaylord Larsen. *Dorothy and Agatha*. New York: Dutton, 1990. 230 pp. $16.95.

A recommendation from someone else about a book usually makes me edgy, uncomfortable, and I began the "faction" book about Dorothy L. Sayers and Agatha Christie with some misgivings. I need not have had those misgivings. *Dorothy and Agatha* is a quick read. The author's note says that he used certain facts about the lives of the two and that the rest is fiction.

Fiction begins with Dorothy L. (never forget the *L;* she would be livid) finds a corpse in her home. She wants to avoid publicity about the matter because she is in the middle of producing a religious play. But several days later, the Detection Club meets, with G. K. Chesterton recently dead (so the year must be 1937). A. A. Milne's wife had seen the newspaper story about the corpse in the Fleming home, and he asks about it. The club decides to help her privately, naming a committee and choosing a reluctant Agatha Christie to be in charge.

Larsen claims that the very different personalities of these leading ladies of mystery have more in common than might be thought. But. Many of the clues are puzzles, and it's surprising but not surprising that it's Agatha's show, especially as she tools around in her car. Although Larsen is not quite accurate in his reference to *Gaudy Night* (p. 78), he plots neatly and gives fair clues. I confess I missed the big one. I blush. Should I do penance by reading *The Kleinart Case?* A swiftee. (Jane Gottschalk)

Jane Haddam (Orania Papazoglou). *Precious Blood.* Bantam, 1991.

This is the second in a series of "Gregor Demarkian Holiday Mysteries." I haven't caught up with the first one, *Not a Creature Was Stirring,* clearly set at Christmastime, so some of the background for the ex-FBI agent, now unlicensed amateur detective, is unclear. That makes little difference, however, for the bulk of the book is set, not in Demarkian's Armenian neighborhood in Philadelphia, but in the town of Colchester in upstate New York.

Demarkian is a widower who retired from the FBI when his wife died and who moved back to his roots. There he hobnobs with close friend, Father Tibor Kasparian, of the Armenian Rite Catholic Church. Father Tibor is a good friend of Roman Catholic Cardinal Archbishop O'Bannion of Colchester, so when a mysterious death which impinges on the lives of prominent members of the archdiocese occurs in Colchester, O'Bannion leans on the priest to get Gregor to come and investigate.

Twenty years earlier a scandal broke upon Colchester; the events at Black Rock Park included what appeared to be the ritual murders of some animals. The people involved were never publicly identified. Now, on Ash Wednesday, one of them has returned to Colchester, anxious to renew her ties with her old friends and, since she's dying of cancer, have a few last happy days reviving the memory of what for her was one of the most joyful times of her pitiful life. Cheryl Cass, 36 and penniless, spent her remaining few dollars on a bus ride home. She intended to die there, but not by murder. Her body was found in an alley, dead of nicotine poisoning. Suicide, said the police.

The Cardinal Archbishop was not satisfied; he would dearly like to link Cheryl Cass's death with a pestiferous priest, Fr. Andy Walsh, parish priest of St. Agnes', right next door to the cathedral. Andy was one of the high-school gang that Cheryl remembered so fondly. The others, like Andy, had gone on to become successful adults in their own chosen ways: Tom Dolan is a priest also, assistant to the Cardinal; Peg Morissey is married and the mother of nine plus one soon to be born; Judy Eagan has a flourishing catering business and is engaged to a rising politician; Kathleen Burke is now Sister Scholastic, principal of the parochial school and on her way to greater things. Only Barry Field has left the fold; he has become rabidly anti-Roman Catholic and has a television-evangelism station, soon to become part of a national network.

Though presumably the holiday is Easter, the action takes place from Ash Wednesday through Good Friday, with another spectacular murder on Holy Thursday. The activities of a conservative Roman Catholic parish during Holy Week are the background for murder and investigation. All of the members of the old gang stand to lose if what Cheryl Cass has to tell becomes public knowledge. But which one has so much to lose that murder is the only way out?

Gregor's Lenten meals of lentils put a little humor into the story, but it is basically a tragedy, compounded of youthful indiscretions and the rigid standards of the Roman Catholic Church. (Maryell Cleary)

www.ingramcontent.com/pod-product-compliance
Lightning Source LLC
Chambersburg PA
CBHW031408040426
42444CB00005B/477